MW01595448

First Things First

A Study in Our Fundamental Faith

Marvin McKenzie

Copyright @2014 Marvin McKenzie

All Scriptures are taken from the King James Bible.

Published in the United States of America

First Things First – an Introduction
Hebrews 5:12

It was the late summer or early spring of 1988 when I received a phone call from Rich Pomeroy. Mr. Pomeroy was then working as the human resource manager for the contractor. They were seeking qualified people to work for them building a 300-foot tall Titan IV rocket launch pad, to be built in Astoria, OR and then shipped to Vandenberg AFB. Rich had hired me three years earlier to work on an oil refinery that we built on the docks in Astoria and was then shipped to Alaska. He was a Christian and had attended our church once.

He knew me, knew where to find me, and knew I was an experienced ironworker. I was the first construction worker hired and led the first "raising Gang" building two of the six sections that completed the launch pad.

The plan was to divide that 300 ft tower into six 50 ft sections. The six sections were then barged to Vandenberg and that stacked, one on top of the other. Each section was approximately 100 ft by 100 feet by 50ft tall. Once the sections were at Vandenberg, the top section was jacked in the air high enough roll the next section under it and the two were bolted together. Then those two were jacked in the air high enough to roll the next section under than so they could be bolted together – and so on.

When a person thinks about it, there are about a half a dozen ways a project like that could go wrong:
- **It was a huge construction project**
- **It was built 900 miles from where it was going to be permanently located**
- **It had to be built in sections rather than as a whole and**

- **It had to be reassembled by a different crew than originally built it.**

There is a trick that helps keep construction projects like that on course; there is one thing that is always constant, and everyone keeps going back to that constant. In the case of the launch pad, we had blueprints.

But we also had something else; an engineer was supervising the project who:
- **Had helped design the launch pad**
- **Had helped draw up the blueprints we all used**
- **Was on site watching us through the entire construction process**
- **Would be at Vandenberg when the sections of the launch pad were assembled and as I understood it**
- **Would oversee the use of the launch pad through its life**

In order to stay on course in life there has to be something that grounds us
- **Something we hold as a constant**
- **Something we keep going back to**
- **Something keeps our bearings on the right path**

You see it everywhere. Denominations like the
- **Old German Lutherans**
- **The early Presbyterians and**
- **The Methodists of early American history**

based their doctrine on the Word of God and their doctrine impacted how they lived.

But then, first in the Lutheran higher criticism and later on in the Presbyterians and finally the Methodists – their religion allowed for
- **More questioning of the Bible which led to**
- **Fewer convictions concerning their doctrine and that led to**
- **An abandonment of Christian lifestyle**

I see it in a good number of Baptist churches too:

- **They question our Bible**
- **They stop teaching much doctrine and finally**
- **They forsake the convictions that have distinguished Baptists for 2000 years**

And unfortunately, it happens to individual Christians. Unless there is
- **Something in our faith that never changes**
- **Something we can hold on to as our anchor**

we will drift further and further off course.

I am confident that we cannot rightly go forward unless we keep a firm hold where we began. So with the Lord's help and blessing, my intention is to go back to those things that ground the believer.

I find three Biblical reasons for doing so:

TO PROVIDE MILK FOR THOSE CHRISTIANS WHO NEED IT

1 Peter 2:2 KJV

As newborn babes, desire the sincere milk of the word, that ye may grow thereby:

Every baby starts with milk. But I still like a good cold glass of it here and there. Most of us never really grow out of it, at least a little. For the Christ these would be
- **The first principles**
- **The foundational doctrines**
- **The fundamentals of the faith**

I see two sorts of people who will benefit from some good solid fundamental doctrine this year: There is of course:

A. The brand-new Christian

Just like a baby is always better off with good healthy milk and not something like cool aide. So a new Christian will be much better off with really good teaching and not a bunch of entertainment.

Then there is
B. The Christian who has been struggling in his faith
1 Corinthians 3:1-2 KJV
And I, brethren, could not speak unto you as unto spiritual, but as unto carnal, even as unto babes in Christ.
I have fed you with milk, and not with meat: for hitherto ye were not able to bear it, neither yet now are ye able.

Paul wrote these words to people who were not babes in Christ, but who had not grown in their faith as they should have.
- **He wrote that these believers came behind in none of the spiritual gifts.**
- **They had benefitted from Paul's presence and ministry for a year and six months, longer than he stayed anywhere else except Ephesus**
- **They had other gifted teachers of the Bible like Apollos**
- **They were apparently a generous church who Paul had set as an example to other churches to encourage them to give**

But they were still, he said carnal, and "as babes." So he said he had to feed them milk and not meat.

Regardless of how long you have been saved then,
- **If you have gotten stuck in your faith –**
- **If you haven't grown for some time,**
- **If it has been a while since you can mark a real change in your life because of Christ,**

the trick is not to get more meat, but more milk.

- **You don't need to hear new things**
- **You need to rehear the fundamental, first things**

- **It might be that you didn't get those first things really grounded well**
- **It might be you missed some of them altogether.**

TO STIR UP THE MEMORY OF THOSE CHRISTIANS WHO HAVE BEEN AT IT A WHILE

2 Peter 1:12-15 KJV
Wherefore I will not be negligent to put you always in remembrance of these things, though ye know them, and be established in the present truth.
Yea, I think it meet, as long as I am in this tabernacle, to stir you up by putting you in remembrance;
Knowing that shortly I must put off this my tabernacle, even as our Lord Jesus Christ hath shewed me.
Moreover I will endeavour that ye may be able after my decease to have these things always in remembrance.

A. Peter knew he wouldn't live forever so he said he wanted to take them back through these fundamental things

- To stir these solid believers up and
- To help them remember these things once he was gone

1. To be stirred up means to excite and arouse them.

You know how we can get when we have been at something for a long time….

- We can forget why we are doing it and
- We can get lazy about how we do it

I just watched a little program about Christopher Columbus with my grandkids a couple weeks ago. It reminded me how just before they reached the West Indies, his crew almost mutinied against him. When they left Spain, they knew they were going on a long and dangerous voyage.
- They were trained sailors
- They were used to long sea voyages
but somehow, after weeks and weeks at sea, they forgot their commitment. That can happen to any of us. Once in a while we need something that reminds us of what we are doing as Christians and why.

Now be honest with yourself and the Lord;

- **Are you as committed to the cause of Christ today as you once were?**
- **Or have you let time and experience settle your soul about spiritual things?**

Peter told these Christians that he wanted to rehearse these things they already knew so he could stir them up and excite them once again about the things of God.

He also said he wanted to teach these things again
2. So that they would remember them after his departure
We are supposed to grow and change as we go along as believers, but our faith is not. What we believe and how we practice it is supposed to stay the same. That's supposed to be the bedrock upon which our growth takes place.

The Bible uses the picture of a building. The building ought to grow and expand, but if you don't keep the building on the foundation it is eventually going to collapse.

I see an awful lot of Christian building going on these days that has left the foundation.
- **Right now it looks good**
- **Right now it seems successful**

but it isn't built right
- **Preachers have departed from the doctrines they promised to proclaim**
- **Churches have strayed from those convictions that have been our distinctives**
- **Christians have waffled on practices that our Baptist forefathers died for instead of compromising**

One day the building they are constructing will collapse around them.

Paul admonished Timothy,
2 Timothy 2:2 KJV
And the things that thou hast heard of me among many witnesses, the same commit thou to faithful men, who shall be able to teach others also.

We're not supposed to learn enough doctrine to strike out on our own and grow past our teachers; we're supposed to learn the things that Paul taught well enough that we can be sure we continue on our present course and so we can teach others to do that same.

Christianity is not supposed to have begun with Christ and the Apostles and "grow up" into something better as the years go on: it is supposed to stay the same:
- **Year after year**
- **Century after century and**
- **Continent to continent**

TO EARNESTLY CONTEND FOR THE FAITH

Jude 1:3-4 KJV

Beloved, when I gave all diligence to write unto you of the common salvation, it was needful for me to write unto you, and exhort you that ye should earnestly contend for the faith which was once delivered unto the saints.

For there are certain men crept in unawares, who were before of old ordained to this condemnation, ungodly men, turning the grace of our God into lasciviousness, and denying the only Lord God, and our Lord Jesus Christ.

A. Jude wanted to write about something else

A true pastor isn't a fighter by nature.

- **He loves people**
- **He wants to see people saved**
- **He wants to be a blessing and a help to everybody**

B. Jude recognized the need for some contention

By the way, this was no mild contention either. He said "*ye should earnestly contend for the faith.*"

This struggle is to be done with vigor and passion. It is, a make or break contest. It's not just a game where one wins, and one loses and both sides shake hands at the end. If this struggle is lost, so are the souls of men. Eventually the very faith Christ and the apostles preached would be gone.

1. Jude was anxious to recruit others in the contest
That is at least part of the reason for this book. I want to get you in the struggle. I want to teach you, if you haven't learned them, and remind you, if you have, of those fundamental doctrines. By doing so, I hope to point out how those doctrines are being jeopardized in our world today. And then get you involved in the contest to preserve them.

2. It is a struggle through conviction and by holding fast our doctrine and not by violence
2 Corinthians 10:4 KJV
(For the weapons of our warfare are not carnal, but mighty through God to the pulling down of strong holds;)

I would never advocate taking up arms or doubling up your fist in the fight we have to fight. Paul said in Ephesians 6:12 KJV *For we wrestle not against flesh and blood, but against principalities, against powers, against the rulers of the darkness of this world, against spiritual wickedness in high places.* So our contest is not directed at anybody.

When it comes to matters of the faith, we should have no quarrel with any man or woman on this planet.
- **Our passion**
- **Our fire**
- **Our earnest heat**

should not be directed at any person because he or she is not the author of our battle.

3. This struggle will involve personalities and names

In verse four, Jude just calls them "certain men." But later on names begin to come up

- **Cain and**
- **Balaam and**
- **Core**

Those are all guys who were long dead in Jude's day.

Paul, who loves to mention the names of people who have been especially helpful to him, is not at all afraid to give the names of those who were contrary to the truth. In the book of Acts we have

- **Simon who had bewitched the people of Samaria[1] and**
- **Elymas the sorcerer who sought to turn Sergius Paulus from the faith[2]**
- **The failure of John Mark who abandoned them in the work[3]**
- **The contention between Paul and Barnabas[4]**
- **The seven sons of Sceva who tried to cast out a demon in Paul's name[5]**

Paul mentions

- **Hymenaus and Alexander who had put away their faith and were shipwrecked spiritually[6]**
- **Philetus was a profane and vain babbler[7]**
- **Demas who had been a fellowservant but who abandoned him, loving this present world[8]**
- **Alexander the coppersmith who had done him much evil[9] and**

Apostle John mentioned

- **Diotrophes who loved to have the preeminence.[10]**

---

[1] Acts 8:9
[2] Acts 13:8
[3] Acts 13:13
[4] Acts 15:39
[5] Acts 19:14
[6] 1 Timothy 1:20
[7] 2 Timothy 2:17
[8] 2 Timothy 4:10
[9] 2 Timothy 4:14
[10] 3 John 1:9

The contest *is not* **violent**, not **hateful** but it *is* **passionate** and **personal**

And then notice
4. It is all about the faith which was once delivered
That brings me back to where we started this thing;
- **The first principles**
- **The foundational truths**
- **The fundamentals**

God being my helper I want to recruit some soldiers of the Lord Jesus Christ who do battle with spiritual wickedness in high places, not through some angry demonstration of the flesh, but
- **By knowing those first principles of the Bible**
- **By standing for them without wavering and**
- **By being teachers of these very things to others also**

Fundamentals Concerning God

Chapter Two
The First Fundamental
Genesis 1:1

I suppose, when addressing the subject of fundamental or first things, it always best to begin at the beginning.

If we cannot answer the subject of God, then there is no reason to try to address the fundamentals of Christian faith.

It would be good for us to remember that, ever since the sin of Adam and Eve, the God question has been raised. It is not new to our day and age. Certainly, the questions concerning God have taken on different languages and various terminologies, but the question of this fundamental doctrine does not begin with our generation. It is a question that has been challenged from the beginning of the sin nature.

IN THE BEGINNING
Genesis 1:1 KJV
In the beginning God created the heaven and the earth.

It has been said one hundred thousand times I guess and can bear to be said one hundred thousand times again. "The Bible presumes the existence of God."
- **There is no explanation for God**
- **There is no account given of God**
- **There is simply God**

In the beginning God…
The degeneration away from the living God began quickly once Adam and Eve had sinned against the Lord. Cain's sin nature is not only revealed in his murder of his brother but

- **In his attitude toward worship "I can give God what I want to give Him" and**
- **In his response to God's confrontation, "Am I my brother's keeper?"**

One doesn't have to look far into the history of mankind to find that man has nearly always challenged

A. The concept of God

I mean by this, whether He is the living God of the Bible or some sort of man-made being.

Lamech thought God was puny enough that he could murder without God's judgment

Genesis 4:23-24 KJV

And Lamech said unto his wives, Adah and Zillah, Hear my voice; ye wives of Lamech, hearken unto my speech: for I have slain a man to my wounding, and a young man to my hurt.
If Cain shall be avenged sevenfold, truly Lamech seventy and sevenfold.[11]

Nimrod thought God was low enough he could build a tower to reach unto heaven

Genesis 11:4 KJV

And they said, Go to, let us build us a city and a tower, whose top may reach unto heaven; and let us make us a name, lest we be scattered abroad upon the face of the whole earth.

---

[11] Matthew Poole writes, "…the sense may be this, Fear not for me; for if any man, though in his youth and strength, should assault me, and give me the first wound, he should pay dearly for it; and though I were wounded and weakened, the remainders of my strength would be sufficient to give him his death's wound. The words also may be otherwise rendered; the particle *chi* being taken interrogatively, as it is Isaiah 29:6, Isaiah 36:19, and elsewhere: *Have I slain a man to my wounding, and or, or a young man to my hurt?* i.e. that thereby I should deserve such a mortal wound or hurt to be inflicted upon me by way of retaliation? You have therefore no cause of fear, either for my sake or for your own.

It wasn't long before men were
- **Carving their gods out of wood or**
- **Fashioning them out of metal**

And when Abraham left the Ur of Chaldees to follow the true and living God, he quickly became a minority in this world. We just have our own versions of those same things today. One person says
- **I don't need God. another says**
- **I don't know if there is a god. While still others say**
- **I have my own gods.**

And those who believe there is a living God that man is accountable to are, as has always been the case, the minority in this world.

If men have challenged the concept of God, they have also questioned

B. The character of God

It began with the seed of rebellion the serpent planted in the heart of Eve:

Genesis 3:4-5 KJV

And the serpent said unto the woman, Ye shall not surely die:
For God doth know that in the day ye eat thereof, then your eyes shall be opened, and ye shall be as gods, knowing good and evil.

Here is a challenge of the very nature of goodness of God.

Now, I contest that every man knows God is.
- **I think he works hard to deny it**
- **I think he has a twisted and contorted view of God**
- **I think he developed ways to explain away God**

But I don't believe there is any such thing as a "real" atheist. There is too much evidence of the existence of God for any man to really not know that God is. But Satan's seed of rebellion has so warped that knowledge of God that the majority of men don't like God. They have decided that they know what is good and what is evil better than God does.

Isn't this the reason why whenever something like the shooting in Connecticut takes place one of the first questions is, "Why would God allow such a thing to happen?"

- **If God is sovereign, why didn't He stop it?**
- **Why does God allow evil things to happen?**

- **Why do I need to go to church?**
- **Why do I need to tithe?**
- **Why should I be a witness?**

Every one of us struggles to some degree with the character of God.

And then there is the question of
C. The creation of God
The question of creation vs evolution did not begin with Darwin, He only pretended to give scientific justification for the belief in evolution. The ancient civilizations of the world all had their nonbiblical explanations for where the world came from.

Some of them were pretty ridiculous Like the 3000-year-old one where two half god half human beings got into a fight:
One killed the other and split the body open
- **From the fluids he made heavens and**
- **From the body he made the earth**
Sounds pretty stupid to our "educated" minds, doesn't it?

Just about as stupid as that a huge explosion happened 300 billion years ago and there was so much energy in the blast that it pounded a bunch of molecules together and they started vibrating with energy – that energy became life. And that life, together with billions of years of accidental mutation, evolved:
- **From the goo**
- **To the zoo and then**
- **To you**

Even the most dogmatic of evolutionary scientists know that could not have happened.

One of the most famous of them, Richard Dawkins, admitted as much on camera in the documentary, **"Expelled, No Intelligence Allowed."** When asked where the microbe of original life came from the, he actually suggested that it might have been "seeded" on this planet billions of years ago by aliens.

Nothing has changed in 3000 years has it? People who question God always come up with strange and ridiculous ways to explain away God.

If God simply declares His existence with no explanation, is there anything we can know about God? In fact there is. God seems to concern Himself with man's knowledge of who He is.

- **He begins to declare Himself to Abraham and**
- **Continues to do so with the nation of Israel**

I think the most intense declaration of Himself is given to the heathen Babylonians through Isaiah.

I WANT YOU TO KNOW
Isaiah 45:5-7 KJV
I am the LORD, and there is none else, there is no God beside me: I girded thee, though thou hast not known me:
That they may know from the rising of the sun, and from the west, that there is none beside me. I am the LORD, and there is none else.
I form the light, and create darkness: I make peace, and create evil: I the LORD do all these things.

This is really a fascinating passage to me because it is Isaiah preaching a message to a man named Cyrus, who won't be alive for another one hundred years. Cyrus is a Persian king, not Babylonian, but his nation defeated the Babylonians and inherited the Jews in Babylonian captivity.

God's message to Cyrus, through Isaiah consists of three points:

A. "I am God"

According to God there is no debating who God is.

- **He is the God of Abraham, Isaac and Jacob**
- **He is the God of the Bible**
- **He is the God who led Israel out of Egypt**
- **He is the God who gave us the Ten Commandments**

Further

B. There is no other god

So, if we will listen to God we can stop debating about the other gods of the world.

- **The god of Islam**
- **The god of Hindi**
- **The god of Buddhism**

are all false gods, a sham, the product of *satanic imagination* and *human invention.*

Isaiah 44:8-10 KJV

Fear ye not, neither be afraid: have not I told thee from that time, and have declared it? ye are even my witnesses. Is there a God beside me? yea, there is no God; I know not any.
They that make a graven image are all of them vanity; and their delectable things shall not profit; and they are their own witnesses; they see not, nor know; that they may be ashamed.
Who hath formed a god, or molten a graven image that is profitable for nothing?

The most important thing God told Cyrus is,

C. I created you

Isaiah 45:9 KJV

Woe unto him that striveth with his Maker! Let the potsherd strive with the potsherds of the earth. Shall the clay say to him that fashioneth it, What makest thou? or thy work, He hath no hands?

The issue of creation comes up over and over again in the Bible. And it is no wonder that those who resist God always resist creation. Creation implies accountability to our Creator. If we are not created, we are free to do what is right in our own eyes. However, if we have a Maker, we have no business striving with Him.

Despite all of man's objections and misconceptions about God, God is. And He has revealed Himself to us in Jesus Christ.

IF YOU HAVE SEEN JESUS
Hebrews 1:1-3 KJV
God, who at sundry times and in divers manners spake in time past unto the fathers by the prophets,
Hath in these last days spoken unto us by his Son, whom he hath appointed heir of all things, by whom also he made the worlds;
Who being the brightness of his glory, and the express image of his person, and upholding all things by the word of his power, when he had by himself purged our sins, sat down on the right hand of the Majesty on high;

There is only one true God. All other gods are the work of man's hands. And the express image of God is the person of Jesus Christ.

Jesus Christ is
A. The express image of God
John 14:8-9 KJV
Philip saith unto him, Lord, shew us the Father, and it sufficeth us.
Jesus saith unto him, Have I been so long time with you, and yet hast thou not known me, Philip? he that hath seen me hath seen the Father; and how sayest thou then, Shew us the Father?

I recall the day when Saul of Tarsus met the Lord on the Damascus road. There he was,
- **A leader of the religious sect of the Pharisees**
- **A zealous practitioner of his faith**

Obviously in the presence of God and his first question was, *"Who art thou Lord?"*

I think a lot of religious people are right there.
- **They may seem confident in their religion**
- **They may appear to be dogmatically opposed to Christianity**

but they may also wish they could know for sure who is God.

Saul asked, *"Who art thou Lord?"* And the Lord answered *"I am Jesus of Nazareth, whom thou persecutest."*

Jesus Christ is
B. The one way to heaven
John 14:6 KJV
Jesus saith unto him, I am the way, the truth, and the life: no man cometh unto the Father, but by me.

Acts 4:12 KJV
Neither is there salvation in any other: for there is none other name under heaven given among men, whereby we must be saved.

- **Jesus is not a way to God**
- **Jesus is not even the best way to God**
- **Jesus is the way**

And there is no other way

C. The author and finisher of our faith
Hebrews 12:2 KJV
Looking unto Jesus the author and finisher of our faith; who for the joy that was set before him endured the cross, despising the shame, and is set down at the right hand of the throne of God.

First Things First, the Fundamentals of Christian faith:
and it all begins right here
- **There is one God and only one**
- **He has revealed Himself in the Person of Jesus Christ**

Jesus is, Colossians 2:9 KJV "*.... all the fulness of the Godhead bodily.*" Everything we need to know about God, we find in Jesus Christ.

Chapter Three
What is God Like?
Jeremiah 9:24 KJV

Nowhere does the Bible attempt to explain God's existence, the very first words of the Book declare, *"In the beginning God..."*

It is inherent, built in us, to know God is.
- **The heavens declare it**
- **The Creation demands it and**
- **The heart knows it**

But the sin of Adam and Eve perverted that understanding of God from the very beginning.
- **The concept of God**
- **The character of God and**
- **The creation of God**

began to come into question. So, the Bible does not attempt to tell us how God came into being, but immediately sets out to tell us who God is.

In Isaiah 45:5-7 KJV God expresses himself through Isaiah to Cyrus, the King of the Persians, who would not even be born for another one hundred years:

I am the LORD, and there is none else, there is no God beside me: I girded thee, though thou hast not known me:
That they may know from the rising of the sun, and from the west, that there is none beside me. I am the LORD, and there is none else.
I form the light, and create darkness: I make peace, and create evil: I the LORD do all these things.

God told Cyrus, this Gentile king, three things about Himself:
- **He is God (the God of Abraham Isaac and Jacob)**
- **There is no other god**
- **He was Cyrus' maker (and as Maker, we are accountable to**

Him)

But the ultimate expression of God was found in the Person of Jesus Christ. Jesus said
John 14:9 KJV
... he that hath seen me hath seen the Father ... So, we know God is and we know who God is.

There is another great question concerning God that keeps cropping up throughout Old Testament history;
What is God Like?

Everything we know about the history of man tells us that men have always, inherently worshiped God. There has never been a question concerning if God is, but since the original sin men have questioned who God is and what is He like.

We find throughout history
MISUNDERSTANDINGS about GOD

They knew God existed, but the sin nature had perverted their understanding of Him.

A. One of the early theories about the creation of the heavens and the earth.
I want to give the story to you just to show how messed up it is.

The story involves the god, Marduk and the goddess Tiamat, the mother of all. It was decided among the other gods that Marduk was to be the head god, but he would have to defeat Tiamut in order to be the ruler of the gods. So Marduk grabbed his Bow and Arrows and a mace and set out to do battle with Tiamat.

Marduk accuses Tiamat and says, **"...Why are you rising,**

your pride vaulting, your heart set on faction, so that sons reject fathers? Mother of all, why did you have to mother war? 'You made that bungler your husband, Kingu! You gave him the rank, not his by right, ... You have abused the gods my ancestors..."

Tiamat turned to Marduk, "... her wits scattered, she was possessed and shrieked aloud, her legs shook from the crotch down, she gabbled spells, muttered maledictions..."

While she was screaming, Marduk sent the god of wind to blow so hard she could not shut her mouth. He blew and blew until she swelled up with all of the air inside of her. It was at this point that Marduk shot his arrow into her belly, splitting her wide open. He threw her down, straddled her dead body and "...smashed her skull (for the mace was merciless)..."

At this point in the story Marduk stops and "...gazed at the huge body, pondering how to use it, what to create from the dead carcass. He split it apart like a cockle-shell..."

With the upper half he made the arc of the sky. With the other half the earthly image.

B. All of the ideas people had about the gods were equally messed up.
They viewed the gods as first of all, many – every country had their own gods and every country had a lot of them.
- **The sun**
- **The river**
- **The earth**
- **The wind**

All of them were gods, and all of them were very angry. They felt like they were constantly at odds with their gods, fighting for some way to keep them happy

- Or else they would get no rain
- Or else a storm would destroy their crops
- Or else an enemy would invade their land
- Or else they would fail when they invaded someone else's land

And they believed the gods could be defeated. Rabshekah said as much to the Jews when he laid siege to Jerusalem.
2 Kings 18:33-35 KJV
Hath any of the gods of the nations delivered at all his land out of the hand of the king of Assyria?
Where are the gods of Hamath, and of Arpad? where are the gods of Sepharvaim, Hena, and Ivah? have they delivered Samaria out of mine hand?
Who are they among all the gods of the countries, that have delivered their country out of mine hand, that the LORD should deliver Jerusalem out of mine hand?

Rabshekah acknowledged these gods existed, but he didn't believe they could defeat him.

C. It's no different modern-day atheists and agnostics

I do not believe it is that they really don't believe. I just think their belief is twisted, perverted. They have a misunderstanding about who God is and what God is like. And those misunderstanding lead them to conclude that God is:

- **Cruel or**
- **Hateful or**
- **Impotent**

Men have misunderstood God since the original sin.

So, God told the prophet Jeremiah

WHAT GOD LIKES

Jeremiah 9:24 KJV
But let him that glorieth glory in this, that he understandeth and knoweth me, that I am the LORD which exercise lovingkindness, judgment, and righteousness, in the earth: for in these things I delight,

saith the LORD.

Tell me what a person enjoys, and I can tell you a great deal about the person. God describes what He is like by telling us what He likes, or delights in. All three of the delights of God are an exercise, an activity.

God delights in exercising
A. Lovingkindness
We should view all that God does as being done out of love.

Jeremiah 12:7 KJV
I have forsaken mine house, I have left mine heritage; I have given the dearly beloved of my soul into the hand of her enemies.

The passage is speaking about the Jews being captured and carried away by Babylon. We, who have read the story, know that God did not give them into the hand of the enemy because He hated them, but because He loved them.

No truly loving parent leaves his child without discipline and training – it is setting them up for a life of misery.

I learned a few interesting things about James and Dolly Madison. Dolly was a widow with one child (and another who had died as an infant) when she married James Madison, who was seventeen years older than she was. They never had any children together, but James was happy to raise her son, Payne, as his own.

Payne grew up spoiled. Dolly would not correct him, James joked about not being able to get him to study. When he grew older then President Madison sent him to England as an aide to an American diplomat, hoping the trip would teach him some responsibility. Instead he went ran off to Paris and fell in with prostitutes there.

He became a huge gambler, but Dolly refused to believe he was a bad boy and Payne drove the then retired President Madison and Dolly into near bankruptcy paying his gambling debts. Dolly could not bear to think her boy was involved in all of that, so James quietly paid the debts without telling her.

When President Madison died, Dolly turned Montpelier, their estate over Payne, who promptly stole everything of value and ran the plantation into the ground. Dolly had to sell it piece by piece and spent twenty years of her life in absolute poverty one of their slaves who had bought his own freedom, would drop by and give her food and other necessities – she was so destitute.

Finally, she moved to Washington DC, where congress agreed to buy James Madison's papers from her on condition that the money be put in a trust to care for her and administered by people who refused to give any of it to Payne. Payne responded by suing the government. (He lost).

He died just two years after his mother
- **He had never married**
- **He had never had a job to speak of**
- **He had wasted his life and His step father's fortune on gambling and drinking**

The historians say that for all of the greatness of James and Dolly Madison, their refusal to discipline Payne was their lifelong Achilles' heel.[12]

God loves us too much to leave us to our own devices

---

[12] **Achilles**: In Greek mythology, the principal hero of the Trojan War, made invulnerable by being dipped in the river Styx as a baby, except for the heel he was held by. He killed the Trojan hero Hector before being fatally wounded in the heel with an arrow fired by Paris.

God delights in exercising
B. Judgment

When you first hear this, it might sound like God delights in judging and condemning people.

But that is not it at all.
In Romans 5:1 KJV we read
Therefore being justified by faith, we have peace with God through our Lord Jesus Christ:

The word justify refers to a judge finding a man not guilty.

God delights, don't you see, in finding you and me not guilty
- **Though we have sinned**
- **Though we are guilty**
- **Though we should be judged**

Because of the death, burial and resurrection of Jesus Christ, any who will believe and call on the name of Jesus Christ are judged *Not Guilty* by God

God delights in exercising
C. Righteousness
He delights in exercising Himself in the cause of purifying for Himself a people zealous of good works.[13]

I would like to give now,
MY ADVICE CONCERNING YOU AND GOD
And that is to follow the example of the Apostle Paul who wrote,
Philippians 3:7-10 KJV
But what things were gain to me, those I counted loss for Christ.
Yea doubtless, and I count all things but loss for the excellency of the knowledge of Christ Jesus my Lord: for whom I have suffered the loss of all things, and do count them but dung, that I may win Christ,

---

[13] Titus 2:14

And be found in him, not having mine own righteousness, which is of the law, but that which is through the faith of Christ, the righteousness which is of God by faith:
That I may know him, and the power of his resurrection, and the fellowship of his sufferings, being made conformable unto his death;

A. God is Personal
By personal I mean that God has qualities like you have.
- **He loves**
- **He sees**
- **He hears**
- **He thinks**

In Jesus Christ that personality is even more pronounced
- **He was in all points tempted like as we are**
- **He was hungry**
- **He was thirsty**
- **He got sleepy**

You can know Him because you were created in His image.

B. God is Intelligent
I mean by this that He is aware of you and your circumstances.
- **He knows your sin**
- **He knows your heart**
- **He knows your desires**

- **When you wanted to do good but did not do it – He knows**
- **When you didn't want to evil but did – He know**

He knows the thoughts and intents of your heart.

You can know Him.

C. God is Present
Acts 17:27 KJV
That they should seek the Lord, if haply they might feel after him, and find him, though he be not far from every one of us:

- **No matter who you are**
- **No matter what you might have done**
- **No matter what you believe you believe**

God is not far from us. And you can know Him.
- **You can know Him as your Saviour**
- **You can know Him as your Heavenly Father**
- **You can know Him as your counselor and comforter**
- **You can know Him as your friend that is closer than a brother**

Come to know Him. Let nothing get in the way of knowing God. And if you know He has saved you – grow in grace and in the knowledge of the Lord and Saviour, Jesus Christ.

Chapter Four
The Interest of God
John 3:16 KJV

As time has progressed, men have become more and more emboldened in their accusations and indictments against God. When Adam and Eve sinned, they believed they became as gods, knowing good and evil. Today men will go so far as to impugn God with evil.

- **"If God is", they will often charge, "why does He allow such terrible things to happen?"**
- **"Does God love us?" And "If He does, why do we go through so many trials in our lives?"**
- **"Why can't we pray to the all powerful loving God and find complete escape from all troubles?"**

It is my desire to demonstrate to you through the Word of God that God does love us. We may not always understand his actions any more than a child understands his loving parents' actions, but the Bible is God's revelation of Himself to us - and proclaims that God loves us.

GOD'S LOVE IS EXCLUSIVELY FOR US
The Bible nowhere, that I am aware of, says God loves any other part of His Creation:
- **The heavens and the earth,**
- **The animals of the earth or even**
- **The angels**

I would not want to say God does not love these - they are His creation.

There is sufficient reason for us to believe that we are to respect His creation as His creation:

A. Adam's first responsibility was to dress and keep the garden.[14]

I take it that is still a God ordained instruction for mankind.

- **I am no environmental extremist, but I do accept that the resources of the earth should be managed and used responsibly.**
- **I think it is wise that we are no longer allowed to throw our trash out our car windows without being fined.**
- **It makes since to me that trees that are cut down be replaced with trees to use again in the future.**

B. I see evidence in the Scripture that we should treat our animals well and kindly.

Proverbs 12:10 KJV

A righteous man regardeth the life of his beast: but the tender mercies of the wicked are cruel.

There is very little reason to treat animals, either domesticated or in the wild cruelly. I see no good purpose in killing off every whale just for the fun of it or fishing a species into extinction. But you are not going to find any place in the Bible where God expresses love for the earth and the created things. Even the angels, which are magnificent creations, are never said to be the object of God's love.

GOD LOVES ISRAEL

Deuteronomy 7:6-7 KJV

For thou art an holy people unto the LORD thy God: the LORD thy God hath chosen thee to be a special people unto himself, above all people that are upon the face of the earth.

The LORD did not set his love upon you, nor choose you, because ye were more in number than any people; for ye were the fewest of all people:

---

[14] Genesis 2:15 KJV

And the LORD God took the man, and put him into the garden of Eden to dress it and to keep it.

The key to this passage is that the Jews were not required to earn God's love. He loved them because He loved them.

The whole history of Israel is a demonstration of God loving the undeserving.

- **Abraham almost immediately disobeyed God in taking his father with Him toward the Promised Land**
- **He lacked faith during a famine and went to Egypt and compounded the problem by lying and saying his wife was his sister**
- **When his wife did not give him the baby God promised, he took another woman and had a child by her.**

After all of that, God still kept His promise to Abraham and Sarah and gave them the promised child and made of them the nation of Israel. Trace their family through the generations and you will see that each generation had their own issues with sin:

- **Isaac copied his father's sin in Egypt and lying about his wife**
- **Jacob stole his brother's birthright**
- **Judah conceived a child by his own daughter in law**
- **Moses killed a man**
- **David had Uriah killed in battle and took his wife**

And those are the good Jews! God set his love upon them despite them and not because of them.

I am not implying that God overlooked their sin. As His beloved children, God chastened them (and is still doing so) for their sin. But God has never stopped loving them because of their sin. He never loved them because they were sinless; He loved them because He loved them.

Now do you suppose that if God would love the Jews unconditionally in all of their sin, He would ever stop loving you because of your sin?

But those are the Jews. Is it possible that God loves the Jews and that He loves no one else? Not at all. The Bible also says,

GOD LOVES THE WORLD
John 3:16 KJV
For God so loved the world, that he gave his only begotten Son, that whosoever believeth in him should not perish, but have everlasting life.

When we carefully read the Bible what we learn is that God has always loved the world - all of the men and women of the world. God's love for the Jews has, from the very beginning been for the purpose of bringing out of them the One who would bless the whole world.

Genesis 12:1-3 KJV
Now the LORD had said unto Abram, Get thee out of thy country, and from thy kindred, and from thy father's house, unto a land that I will shew thee:
And I will make of thee a great nation, and I will bless thee, and make thy name great; and thou shalt be a blessing:
And I will bless them that bless thee, and curse him that curseth thee: and in thee shall all families of the earth be blessed.

God's love for all men may be seen as early as the Creation of Adam and Eve
Genesis 1:27 KJV
So God created man in his own image, in the image of God created he him; male and female created he them.

Genesis 2:7 KJV
And the LORD God formed man of the dust of the ground, and breathed into his nostrils the breath of life; and man became a living soul.

- **He created man in the image of God**
- **He created man by breathing into him His very life and**
- **He created the woman from the rib of Adam**

In each case these are loving gestures. He could have just said the word and Adam and Eve would have been there - another one of the animals. Not so. Man was the object of God's love from the moment He created them. The sin of Adam and Eve had in no way shocked God.

A lot of people think they could have better than God did, but God's love for mankind compelled Him to give man the right of free will. Without it, we would be no different that the monkeys. But free will is costly. It meant that the very being God created to love had to have the opportunity to turn away from God's love. So,
- **God gave man a free will**
- **God allowed man to choose Satan over God and**
- **God planned a way to bring man back to His fellowship.**

- **It started with one - Abraham**
- **It grew into a multitude - Israel so that from it**
- **From them came one - Jesus Christ**
- **Who would then "*take(th) away the sin of the world*"**

GOD LOVES JESUS CHRIST
Matthew 3:16-17 KJV
And Jesus, when he was baptized, went up straightway out of the water: and, lo, the heavens were opened unto him, and he saw the Spirit of God descending like a dove, and lighting upon him:
And lo a voice from heaven, saying, This is my beloved Son, in whom I am well pleased.

It is not difficult for me to understand God's love for Jesus Christ
- **They have existed eternally together**
- **They are of the same essence and truth**
- **He is the only begotten of the Father**

I keep a list of people that I love. I take the time to think about it and dwell on those who I love
- **Some of them are my extended family**

- **Most of them are those who have become my spiritual (church) family**

But the love that I have for my immediate family is hard to explain.
- **The kind of love I have for Anita**
- **The way I love Bohannan and Caleb**

it's in a class all by itself.

God's love for Jesus must be a thousand times more pronounced than that love I have for my sons. And yet the Bible says John 3:16 KJV
For God so loved the world, that he gave his only begotten Son, ...

In Romans 8:32 KJV
He that spared not his own Son, but delivered him up for us all, how shall he not with him also freely give us all things?

God loved the world so much that He would not even withhold the greatest object of His love - His only begotten Son. So that if we, in the middle of our sin, would only believe on Him, we would be saved to condemnation and have eternal life.

What about this love?
What should be our response to such great love of God for you and for me?

1 John 4:19 KJV
We love him, because He first loved us.

Love God. Turn to Him with all of your
- **Heart and**
- **Soul and**
- **Strength and**
- **Mind**

Never mind that you do not believe you can love Him as He loves you. Come to Him because He loves you. And as you grow in your knowledge of Him, you will grow also in your love for Him.

CHRIST LOVES THE CHURCH
Ephesians 5:25 KJV
Husbands, love your wives, even as Christ also loved the church, and gave himself for it;

- **God loved the world and gave his Son for it**
- **Christ loved the church Himself for it**

We use this passage to teach on the marriage, but we have the text reversed when we do that. We are supposed to use marriage to teach about Jesus and His love for the church.

This answers to what a Christian is to do with His life after being saved. Since Christ loved the church enough to give His life for it, should we, who have been saved through His **death**, **burial** and **resurrection**, not give as much?

Chapter Five

What About Wrath?
Romans 1:13-18 KJV

If there were no God, faith would be for naught. But we know God is. He has written a conviction of His existence in our hearts. So, we have established in an earlier chapter, Who God is;

- **He is the God of Abraham and Isaac and Jacob**
- **He is the God who is described for us in the Bible and**
- **He is the God whose express image in Jesus Christ**

In the last chapter I described What God is like by showing you what God likes. God delights in exercising

- **Lovingkindness,**
- **Judgment and**
- **Righteousness.**[15]

What About Wrath?

THE FACT OF GOD'S WRATH

Our world is filled with people who have developed their own ideas about whether there is or isn't a God, and if He is, what He must be like. We constantly hear people say

- **God would never send someone to hell**
- **God would never judge someone's sexual orientation**
- **God would never judge someone's lifestyle choices**
- **God would never want a woman to carry a baby she did not want to full term**

---

[15] Jeremiah 9:24 KJV
But let him that glorieth glory in this, that he understandeth and knoweth me, that I am the LORD which exercise lovingkindness, judgment, and righteousness, in the earth: for in these things I delight, saith the LORD.

Each one of those opinions is predicated upon the belief that we choose for ourselves what is good and evil, in other words, we get to create a god who conforms to our image, not the other way around. Whether people today want to accept it or not, God is wrathful. Old Testament and New, even the most casual reading of the Bible bears it out; the very God whose object of love is man, also pours out His wrath upon men.

A. Consider, for instance, the cases of Noah's flood and Sodom and Gomorrah

The word wrath is not used in either of those accounts, but the subject of wrath is certainly demonstrated.

Genesis 6:1-8 KJV

And it came to pass, when men began to multiply on the face of the earth, and daughters were born unto them,
That the sons of God saw the daughters of men that they were fair; and they took them wives of all which they chose.
And the LORD said, My spirit shall not always strive with man, for that he also is flesh: yet his days shall be an hundred and twenty years.
There were giants in the earth in those days; and also after that, when the sons of God came in unto the daughters of men, and they bare children to them, the same became mighty men which were of old, men of renown.
And GOD saw that the wickedness of man was great in the earth, and that every imagination of the thoughts of his heart was only evil continually.
And it repented the LORD that he had made man on the earth, and it grieved him at his heart.
And the LORD said, I will destroy man whom I have created from the face of the earth; both man, and beast, and the creeping thing, and the fowls of the air; for it repenteth me that I have made them.
But Noah found grace in the eyes of the LORD.

- **That God chose to destroy "*man whom [He had] created*"**
- **That God chose to destroy the very object of His love**

is a topic worthy of your contemplation. Praise God that one found grace in the eyes of the Lord.[16]

In the case of Sodom and Gomorrah, the incense of God at the sin of the place is such that the Bible says,
Genesis 18:20-21 KJV
And the LORD said, Because the cry of Sodom and Gomorrah is great, and because their sin is very grievous;
I will go down now, and see whether they have done altogether according to the cry of it, which is come unto me; and if not, I will know.

God chose to see it personally, not just to know it *omnisciently*, but to experience it *physically*, before destroying these places.

In Numbers 16:1-33 KJV and man named Korah led in a rebellion against Moses, resulting in the wrath of God being poured out upon him. The account reads
Now Korah, the son of Izhar, the son of Kohath, the son of Levi, and Dathan and Abiram, the sons of Eliab, and On, the son of Peleth, sons of Reuben, took men:
...
And they gathered themselves together against Moses and against Aaron, and said unto them, Ye take too much upon you, seeing all the congregation are holy, every one of them, and the LORD is among them: wherefore then lift ye up yourselves above the congregation of the LORD?
And when Moses heard it, he fell upon his face:
...
And Moses said unto Korah, Hear, I pray you, ye sons of Levi:
Seemeth it but a small thing unto you, that the God of Israel hath separated you from the congregation of Israel, to bring you near to himself to do the service of the tabernacle of the LORD, and to stand before the congregation to minister unto them?
...
And Moses said unto Korah, Be thou and all thy company before the LORD, thou, and they, and Aaron, to morrow:

---

[16] Not that Noah was worthy of God's grace, but that God was gracious to one who was unworthy.

...

And Moses rose up and went unto Dathan and Abiram; and the elders of Israel followed him.

And he spake unto the congregation, saying, Depart, I pray you, from the tents of these wicked men, and touch nothing of theirs, lest ye be consumed in all their sins.

...

And Moses said, Hereby ye shall know that the LORD hath sent me to do all these works; for I have not done them of mine own mind.

If these men die the common death of all men, or if they be visited after the visitation of all men; then the LORD hath not sent me.

But if the LORD make a new thing, and the earth open her mouth, and swallow them up, with all that appertain unto them, and they go down quick into the pit; then ye shall understand that these men have provoked the LORD.

And it came to pass, as he had made an end of speaking all these words, that the ground clave asunder that was under them:

And the earth opened her mouth, and swallowed them up, and their houses, and all the men that appertained unto Korah, and all their goods.

They, and all that appertained to them, went down alive into the pit, and the earth closed upon them: and they perished from among the congregation.

B. Or in the New Testament

As early as Matthew 3:1-7 KJV

In those days came John the Baptist, preaching in the wilderness of Judaea,

And saying, Repent ye: for the kingdom of heaven is at hand.

...

Then went out to him Jerusalem, and all Judaea, and all the region round about Jordan,

And were baptized of him in Jordan, confessing their sins.

But when he saw many of the Pharisees and Sadducees come to his baptism, he said unto them, O generation of vipers, who hath warned you to flee from the wrath to come?

Through to 2 Thessalonians 1:7-10 KJV

And to you who are troubled rest with us, when the Lord Jesus shall be revealed from heaven with his mighty angels,

In flaming fire taking vengeance on them that know not God, and that obey not the gospel of our Lord Jesus Christ:

Who shall be punished with everlasting destruction from the presence of the Lord, and from the glory of his power;
When he shall come to be glorified in his saints, and to be admired in all them that believe (because our testimony among you was believed) in that day.

I read a great thought concerning this. Knowing the wrath of God; knowing that God is just means I am able to forgive even the worst of my offenders. I am free to love my enemies and bless those who do me harm because I am confident that no unrighteousness will go unanswered.

All the way through the Old Testament and New we see this obvious and completely inescapable fact. There is such a thing as the wrath of God.

- **God makes no apologies for it**
- **God makes no excuses for it**
- **God is in no way embarrassed by it**

THE "KIND" OF GOD'S WRATH
Romans 2:5 KJV
But after thy hardness and impenitent heart treasurest up unto thyself wrath against the day of wrath and revelation of the righteous judgment of God;

One of the reasons that people tend to "judge" the wrath of God is because we have a perverted and personal view of wrath. Almost without exception, when a man becomes filled with wrath, it is a wicked and sinful thing.

- **We know it is wicked when we are wrathful**
- **We sense the wickedness when others are wrathful**

One definition of wrath is "retribution for a perceived wrong." And we know it is wrong to get even, don't we?

I watched a documentary on the Trail of Tears, when the Cherokee Indians were driven off of their land in what is now Georgia.

As the events played out a powerful family among the Cherokees, led by a man whose name was "The Ridge." The whites called him Major Ridge, saw the handwriting on the wall and urged the Cherokee people to surrender to the people of Georgia and move to Oklahoma.

In an effort to save his people, he agreed to lead them to the Oklahoma Territory. But the Indians did not want to go, the majority of them rejected Major Ridge's plan and refused to leave.

- **Those who did go were compensated for the trip and given money to build houses and churches and plant crops.**
- **Those who refused to go were eventually forced out anyway, but when they left, they went without help. More than a quarter of them died as they walked through snow, the 1500 miles.**

The Indians blamed Major Ridge and his family. On the documentary, an expert witness of Indian culture said that the blood of those who had died on the trail had to be avenged. In one day, the Cherokee people murdered Major Ridge, his son, and a nephew. His son John was dragged out of his house and in the presence of his wife and mother, stabbed, hatched, and jumped on until his chest caved in.

It doesn't take much thinking to know that was wicked. The problem is, we usually always define wrath and wicked, and therefore the wrath of God must be wicked too.

Not so, if we accept the Bible as true.
Romans 3:5-6 KJV
But if our unrighteousness commend the righteousness of God, what shall we say? Is God unrighteous who taketh vengeance? (I speak as a man)
God forbid: for then how shall God judge the world?

Let me make just three comments concerning righteousness of God's wrath

A. God's wrath is never mean spirited or hateful

God does not act out of a hateful way but His wrath is always founded in His attribute of love.

- **We have all heard the philosophical question, "Which came first, the chicken or the egg?"**
- **There is a similar theological question that is beaten about by the different schools of faith, "Which came first, the love of God or His justice?"**

In other words,

- **Is God just first, and then loving? Is His love conditioned on justice? Or**
- **Is God loving first and then just?**

The answer is "God is equally both at the same time."

But I would have you to think about this, **Did God create man so He could execute wrath upon him, or did He create man so He could express love toward him?**

I think it is obvious that the reason He created man was so He could love him.

- **He is not mean spirited toward us**
- **He is loving toward us**

and His wrath is poured out always from a heart of love

B. God's wrath is always just and right

A civilized society always establishes:

- **A system of laws and**
- **A means of enforcement**

No civilized people could operate without them. But it is a well-known fact that some man-made laws are immoral and too often mistakes are made in the enforcement of those laws.

- **Innocent people go to jail**

- **Laws are enacted that are later embarrassingly obvious that they are wrong[17]**

Also consider that

C. The lack of wrath on God's would be injustice

Jeremiah 9:4-9 KJV

Take ye heed every one of his neighbour, and trust ye not in any brother: for every brother will utterly supplant, and every neighbour will walk with slanders.

And they will deceive every one his neighbour, and will not speak the truth: they have taught their tongue to speak lies, and weary themselves to commit iniquity.

Thine habitation is in the midst of deceit; through deceit they refuse to know me, saith the LORD.

Therefore thus saith the LORD of hosts, Behold, I will melt them, and try them; for how shall I do for the daughter of my people?

Their tongue is as an arrow shot out; it speaketh deceit: one speaketh peaceably to his neighbour with his mouth, but in heart he layeth his wait.

Shall I not visit them for these things? saith the LORD: shall not my soul be avenged on such a nation as this?

Can't you see what God's is reasoning in this passage? How could God ignore these sins? How could it possibly be right that millions of people have been slain and otherwise horribly abused for nothing more than believing the message of the Bible? If a person refuses to believe, that is their own right. But they do not merely disbelieve, they force their own beliefs on others, and violate those whose faith they revile.

---

[17] I am thinking about the Salem witch trials. Today we know how wrong it is to try a person for such a thing, but we also know that those who were tried and even executed were done so by a system that was completely fraught with flaws. A few very impressionable girls, most of them teenagers, were at first filled with fear of their own punishment and then filled with a sense of power at their ability to accuse anybody and everybody and be believed almost unquestionably. Our nation's concept of justice, previously unheard of in the world, that a man is innocent until proven guilty stems in a large part from the lessons learned in this horrible mark in our history.

It is absolutely consistent with all that is right and just for God to visit His wrath upon men for these crimes.

THE AIM OF GOD'S WRATH
Is that men would ultimately escape it.

2 Peter 3:7-9 KJV
But the heavens and the earth, which are now, by the same word are kept in store, reserved unto fire against the day of judgment and perdition of ungodly men.
But, beloved, be not ignorant of this one thing, that one day is with the Lord as a thousand years, and a thousand years as one day.
The Lord is not slack concerning his promise, as some men count slackness; but is longsuffering to us-ward, not willing that any should perish, but that all should come to repentance.

In the face of such fiery judgment the Bible exclaims that God withholds His wrath, waiting with longsuffering because He is not willing that any should perish. He wants no one to be lost. But there is this caveat; a man will perish if he does not come to final repentance and faith in Jesus Christ as His shelter from the wrath that is to come.

- **Will you come to Jesus Christ?**
- **Will you confess to Him your sin?**
- **Will you trust Him alone to save you from the wrath that is sure to come?**

Chapter Six

Where is God in all This?
1 Timothy 6:15[18]

I think we have this idea

- **That at one time in history every day was another miracle from God.**
- **That at one time, all you had to do was to ask and every need was supplied**
- **That at one time God showed up with amazing demonstrations of miracles and power**

But when we really begin to think about what we have in the Bible, basically four thousand years of history, what we discover is that those periods of time when amazing miracles happened were few and relatively brief. With only a few small exceptions all of the huge miracles in the Bible happened under

- **Moses**
- **Elijah and Elisha**
- **Jesus and the Apostles**

Probably a combined total of less than 100 years of miracles in a four-thousand-year period of time.

The Bible says we walk by faith, not by sight. Christian faith as well as Jewish faith has always been one of believing God through the day to day life and not just when God is raining lightning bolts onto Mount Sinai.

I have been a Christian since 1977. I can testify that during that time God has done some things that were

- **Unquestionable**
- **Undeniable and**
- **Simply amazing**

---

[18] Message originally by John Henry Theisen, 2001

There have been times when Anita and I have sat down together and agreed that it was like we were in a dream.

- **When God gave us a building in Astoria**
- **When God paid the building off without our money or asking anybody for money**
- **When God gave me this church**

But to tell you the truth, most of these 36 years have been just getting up each day and trying to be faithful.

- **Some of those days have been very hard**
- **Some of them have been not boring, but not exciting either**

A lot of them have been going to church praying for and longing for a miracle but being content with the joy of being with God's people even when a revival did not break out.

- **Where is God in the doldrums of day to day life?**
- **Where is God in the common tasks of making a living?**
- **Where is God in the hardships of loss and pain that we so frequently feel?**
- **Where is God in the unfair tragedies that happen too often in this world?**

God is here,
CONTROLLING ALL THINGS.

A. He is controlling all people, nations, events, and circumstances.

- **God is in the rain as well as the sunshine?**
  (No rain during picnic "God was so good to us.")[19]
  God is good even when it pours down rain on the picnic!
- **God is in the natural disasters & other tragedies?**
  (Plane crashes / Fires / Hurricanes)

---

[19] Being a pastor in the Pacific Northwest has given me plenty of occasions to ask God to keep back the rain. More times than I can recall I have asked God to give us good weather and have seen Him answer. For VBS, for Saturday visitation, etc. But there have been more times than that when it rained on my parade.

A few years back a well-intentioned man was trying to get the wording changed on some type of legislation that referred to hurricanes and storms as "acts of God." Are they acts of God?

- **Does God have any control over hurricanes and natural disasters? Like Katrina, Sandy, Hugo?**

Psalms 33:10-11
The LORD bringeth the counsel of the heathen to nought: he maketh the devices of the people of none effect.
The counsel of the LORD standeth for ever, the thoughts of his heart to all generations. (KJV)

B. It's easy to believe God is in control of everything when things are pleasant & going our way.
But it gets much harder to accept that God is in control when we face terrible trials and afflictions.

Several years ago a man named Rabbi Kushner wrote a bestselling book called, *When Bad things Happen to Good People.* The basic theme of book was: "God is EITHER totally sovereign, or totally good, but He CANNOT BE BOTH."

But the Bible says that God is
- **Totally in control (sovereign) and**
- **Totally good at all times**

When everything feels like it is falling apart, God is still in control.
- **God is still on His throne, the sovereign ruler over all the world**
- **He is effecting His will among the nations of the earth and**
- **He is in the midst of us and is in control of whatever is our trial or circumstances**

If there is ANYTHING outside of His control, then He is not the All-knowing, All-Powerful, Everywhere-present God that He claims to be in the Bible.

Some people simply cannot accept that anything difficult or unpleasant or bad could possibly come from or be allowed by a God who loves us.

Not so Joseph
- **His brothers sold him as a slave**
- **His master's wife falsely accused him and had him thrown into prison**

Twenty years later Joseph was the second in command of Egypt and his brother come to him seeking food. They were terrified what he would do to them. Joseph loved them and testified,

Genesis 50:20 KJV

But as for you, ye thought evil against me; but God meant it unto good, to bring to pass, as it is this day, to save much people alive.

Then there was Job
A rich man, Job lost everything in a matter of hours
- **His wealth stolen**
- **His children were slain**
- **His body was afflicted**

Job wrote
Job 13:15 KJV

Though he slay me, yet will I trust in him: but I will maintain mine own ways before him.

Believe me, there have been many days where I have gotten through the day only because I lived quoting that verse.

Job did not see His God through His circumstances, but rather his circumstances through His God.

God is here today, controlling the circumstances.

God is here
COMFORTING HIS CHILDREN
Psalms 18:1-3 KJV
I will love thee, O LORD, my strength.
The LORD is my rock, and my fortress, and my deliverer; my God, my strength, in whom I will trust; my buckler, and the horn of my salvation, and my high tower.
I will call upon the LORD, who is worthy to be praised: so shall I be saved from mine enemies.

We often think of David as one of those men who had special treatment from God. David was favored of the Lord. But David also lived much of his life struggling.
- **He had to flee King Saul**
- **He had to lose his friend Jonathan**
- **He had to fight the Philistines**

David got through his trying times
- **Through prayer and**
- **Through meditation on the Word of God**

He often sang his prayers to the Lord and those songs are recorded for us in the book of Psalms.

Despite the hardships he experienced, David believed that God was there, comforting Him in his time of trouble.
He says God gave him:
A. Strength
Psalms 18:1 KJV
I will love thee, O LORD, my strength.

- **Strength to fight the good fight**
- **Strength to go on when another would have quit**
- **Strength to be thankful when it would have been easy to be bitter**

He says God gave him:
B. Stability
Psalms 18:2 KJV

The LORD is my rock, and my fortress, and my deliverer; my God, my strength, in whom I will trust; my buckler, and the horn of my salvation, and my high tower.

In times of trouble and a Christian remembers
Psalms 18:31 KJV
For who is God save the LORD? or who is a rock save our God?

There is no security, no stability, no foundation other than God.

He says God gave him:
C. Safety
Psalms 18:2 KJV
The LORD is my rock, and my fortress, and my deliverer; my God, my strength, in whom I will trust; my buckler, and the horn of my salvation, and my high tower.

1. David calls God as his **"fortress"**
Which is a place of protection

2. David calls God his **"buckler"**
The Hebrew word comes from the hide of a crocodile.

It's like the armor a soldier would where into battle. Tough and nails, and nothing can get through it.

3. David Calls God his **"high tower"**

A high tower provides not only protection, but perspective.

God helps us to understand
- **Where our problems come from**
- **Why our problems happen and**
- **How our problems may be resolved**

He says God gave him:
D. Salvation

Psalms 18:3 KJV
I will call upon the LORD, who is worthy to be praised: so shall I be saved from mine enemies.

The context here is speaking of a different salvation than going to heaven; it is speaking about being saved from our troubles. God does not keep us from trials and temptations, but He does give us a way of escape that we may be able to bear it. In other words, He gives us comfort in the midst of our trials – if we will receive it.

Where is God today? He is here,
Controlling all things
Comforting His Children

He is here
CALLING OUT TO SINNERS to be saved
Luke 19:10 KJV
For the Son of man is come to seek and to save that which was lost.

The Bible says that death is one appointment we all have to keep.

Most people don't want to think about it, but it is not wise to put off the most certain of certainties...that we will die & stand before God. The Bible is clear: *The only hope we have to be saved is to believe the gospel message and trust in the Lord Jesus Christ while we are alive on this earth*

- **There are no second chances.**
- **There is no back door to heaven**
- **There is no alternative choice**

That is why the Bible says,
Isaiah 55:6-7
Seek ye the LORD while he may be found, call ye upon him while he is near:

Let the wicked forsake his way, and the unrighteous man his thoughts: and let him return unto the LORD, and he will have mercy upon him; and to our God, for he will abundantly pardon. (KJV)

Are you ready to face God? Right now, He's calling.

In Acts chapter 26 the Apostle Paul was preaching to the Roman Governor Festus and the Jewish King Agrippa.
- **He told them how he had met Christ**
- **He told how Jesus was the promised Messiah and**
- **He told them how Christ had risen from the dead**
- **He told them that they could be saved too if they would believe**

Paul pled for them to be saved and in response King Agrippa said
Acts 26:28 KJV
... Almost thou persuadest me to be a Christian.

To which Paul replied
Acts 26:29 KJV
And Paul said, I would to God, that not only thou, but also all that hear me this day, were both almost, and altogether such as I am, except these bonds.

I am trying to persuade you
- **That God is**
- **That God is always good and**
- **That you can trust Him**

Don't be almost persuaded. Don't hear the message and think it sounds right and walk away without the Lord in your life. **If you have never been saved** – don't leave here without asking Christ to forgive your sins and save you. **If you are a Christian** – don't let another day go by without total surrender to the will of the Lord for your life as you find it in the Bible.

Fundamentals Concerning the Bible

Chapter Seven
God Gave Us His Word
2 Timothy 3:16-17 KJV

It is very likely that the most aggressive attack that has ever been faced by Christians has been the attack on the Bible.

It makes a lot of sense from the spiritual point of view.
- **If the Bible is true, then there is a supernatural devil who hates everything that comes from God**
- **If the Bible is true, then every other religion in the world is false**
- **If the Bible is true, then it is the only source of direction to come to know God and His way of salvation**

The Bible has liberated the souls of those who have read for themselves and come to accept the message that it brings. And for that reason, those who have longed to keep men in bondage have striven to keep men from the Bible.

The bedrock of the Christian faith rests upon God. But fixed closely to that is the Word of God because everything we know about God comes,
- **Not from the opinions of gifted men**
- **Not from the evolution of theological though**
- **Not from the process of synods and diets**

The Bible we hold in our hands today boldly professes itself to have come to us through the inspiration of God. I hope to impress upon your minds that your Bible is the product of the inspiration of God.

The Bible declares itself to be something else.
All Scripture is given by inspiration of God….

The Greek word used in this passage is one that literally means **"God breathed."**

It is defined further for us in
2 Peter 1:19-21 KJV
We have also a more sure word of prophecy; whereunto ye do well that ye take heed, as unto a light that shineth in a dark place, until the day dawn, and the day star arise in your hearts:
Knowing this first, that no prophecy of the scripture is of any private interpretation.
For the prophecy came not in old time by the will of man: but holy men of God spake as they were moved by the Holy Ghost.

This is in contrast to what was a popular idea in the days of the ancient Greeks. They would have used a different word for inspiration, eudaimonia... Which means literally **"possessed with a good spirit."**

I have been reading the Fundamentalist Papers, written in the early 1900's to combat the rise of modernistic Christianity which teaches that the Bible is a religious document similar to
- **The Koran or even**
- **The book of Mormon or the Jehovah's Witnesses**
- **The Pearl of Great Price**

which are in merely man-made religious literature.

In one of the Fundamentalist Papers, Dr James Orr wrote in the Bible it is "believed, is a volume which is an inspired record of the whole will of God for man's salvation:
- **Accept as true and inspired the teaching of that book**
- **Follow its guidance and**
- **You cannot stumble**

You cannot err in finding salvation, in grasping the prize of a glorious immortality."[20]

---

[20] Fundamentals, Volume 1 Chapter 5, page 76

Allow me to bring to your attention three main ideas.

The Bible is...
EVIDENCE OF A GOD WHO IS
The phrase "**Thus saith the Lord**" is found 413 times.

The first of them being
Exodus 4:22
And thou shalt say unto Pharaoh, Thus saith the Lord, Israel is my son, even my firstborn:

And the last being
Malachi 1:4
Whereas Edom saith, We are impoverished, but we will return and build the desolate places; thus saith the Lord of hosts, They shall build, but I will throw down; and they shall call them, The border of wickedness, and, The people against whom the Lord hath indignation for ever.

The phrase "**The Word of the Lord**" is found 255 times

The first one,
Genesis 15:1
After these things the word of the Lord came unto Abram in a vision, saying, Fear not, Abram: I am thy shield, and thy exceeding great reward.

The last one being
1 Peter 1:25
But the word of the Lord endureth for ever. And this is the word which by the gospel is preached unto you.

The phrase "**God said**" is found 46 times
The phrase "**My Word**" is found 14 times

These passages assure us that this Bible *is the Word of God.*

More than merely an ideal; we have a heaven-sent message before us.

- **We don't call it the Word of God because that is how we think of it**
- **We call it the Word of God because it declares itself to be the words that God has spoken to men**

But anybody with little character could have written something and claimed that what he wrote was the Word of God.

- **How do we know that the Bible is really the word of God?**
- **How do we know that these holy men of God were moved by the Holy Ghost?**

The Bible is a...

DEMONSTRATION OF A GOD WHO HAS

Deuteronomy 18:19-22 KJV

And it shall come to pass, that whosoever will not hearken unto my words which he shall speak in my name, I will require it of him.

But the prophet, which shall presume to speak a word in my name, which I have not commanded him to speak, or that shall speak in the name of other gods, even that prophet shall die.

And if thou say in thine heart, How shall we know the word which the LORD hath not spoken?

When a prophet speaketh in the name of the LORD, if the thing follow not, nor come to pass, that is the thing which the LORD hath not spoken, but the prophet hath spoken it presumptuously: thou shalt not be afraid of him.

Things were not so different four thousand years ago than they are today.

The question is a valid one. If God is going to use men to tell us what God has said, how do we know if it is really from God, or just someone saying that God spoke to them?

And, by the way, it happened very often that someone presumed to speak for God when they had really not heard from God.[21]

So, God gave them a test….
We will know if the prophet is really from God if everything he prophecies comes to pass exactly how he described it.

That is why all of the major prophecies of the Old Testament have more than one fulfillment
- **One, a near fulfillment, to prove it is from God**
- **The other, more distant, but more important to God's eternal plan**

It gets confusing, but it is important when we study the Old Testament prophets to
- **Understand the near fulfillment – because it proves he is from God and then**
- **Understand and believe, the more distant fulfillment, some of which have not been fulfilled to this day.**

The Bible is filled with prophecies that are there to demonstrate and to prove to us that this book is the very Word of God. According to *The Complete Book of Bible Prophecy*[22] twenty seven percent of the Bible is prophecy and twenty percent of the books of the Bible are prophetic in nature. Of the some 2500 prophecies that are in the Bible, at least 2000 of them have already been fulfilled 100 percent accurately.

---

[21] Jeremiah 28:15-17 KJV
Then said the prophet Jeremiah unto Hananiah the prophet, Hear now, Hananiah; The LORD hath not sent thee; but thou makest this people to trust in a lie.
Therefore thus saith the LORD; Behold, I will cast thee from off the face of the earth: this year thou shalt die, because thou hast taught rebellion against the LORD.
So Hananiah the prophet died the same year in the seventh month.
[22] http://files.tyndale.com/thpdata/FirstChapters/978-0-8423-1831-0.pdf, accessed 2-7-13

Many of the prophecies of the Bible contain such detail and were fulfilled so accurately that many of the skeptics in the academic world have just shrugged them off and said they have to have been written after the fact.

- **Too many details with**
- **Too specific fulfillment**

Can only mean one of two things

- **Either there is a God in heaven who spoke through these Holy men**
- **Or the Bible is a fake**

Some of those prophecies are

- **The scattering of the Jewish nation**
- **The regathering of the Jewish nation**

- **That Judah would be the royal family of Israel**

- **That Jesus would be born in Bethlehem**
- **That Bethlehem would experience a tragic loss of her children**

- **That Jesus would die with transgressors**
- **That Jesus would be so abused that his bones would become dislocated but**
- **That Jesus would be killed without having a bone broken**
- **The Jesus would be buried in a borrowed tomb of a rich man**

Isaiah prophesied that a man named Cyrus would release the Jews from captivity more than 100 years before they went into captivity.

Jeremiah prophesied at the beginning of Babylonian captivity that it would last 70 years.

Daniel prophesied that there would be four major Gentile world empires

- **Babylon**
- **Medo-Persia**
- **Greece and**
- **Rome**

History confirms that there have been those four and only those four world empires.

Rome didn't fall to a greater nation as had happened in earlier conquests. Rome disintegrated from within, dividing first in two and then fragmenting into nothingness.

- **French Napoleon tried to create an empire**
- **Germany's Hitler tried too**

Interestingly, none of the worlds 26 other major religious books try their hand at prophecy.[23]

In Isaiah 41:21-24 KJV God challenges the world…
Produce your cause, saith the LORD; bring forth your strong reasons, saith the King of Jacob.
Let them bring them forth, and shew us what shall happen: let them shew the former things, what they be, that we may consider them, and know the latter end of them; or declare us things for to come.
Shew the things that are to come hereafter, that we may know that ye are gods: yea, do good, or do evil, that we may be dismayed, and behold it together.
Behold, ye are of nothing, and your work of nought: an abomination is he that chooseth you.

Here is how you prove something is from God or not; let them show you what will happen in the future. If they can't do that, they are nothing.

As I said, the Bible contains approximately 2500 prophecies. Of these, 2000 have already been fulfilled. That leaves us with about 500 that have yet to be fulfilled. What about them?

---

[23] http://www.bibleevidences.com/prophecy.htm, accessed 2-7-13

The Bible is a...
PROMISE OF A GOD WHO WILL
2 Peter 3:9 KJV
The Lord is not slack concerning his promise, as some men count slackness; but is longsuffering to us-ward, not willing that any should perish, but that all should come to repentance.

That 2000 Bible promises have been fulfilled exactly as God has given them means that we may confidently consider the remaining prophecies as promises from God. There are five hundred of them and I do not mean to go through them all; but I do want to give those that are most appropriate for you and me today.

The Promise of
A. Sins forgiven
John 1:29 KJV
The next day John seeth Jesus coming unto him, and saith, Behold the Lamb of God, which taketh away the sin of the world.

Matthew 1:21 KJV
And she shall bring forth a son, and thou shalt call his name JESUS: for he shall save his people from their sins.

This is the main focus of everything that is written in the Bible.
- **All of the Mosaic Laws**
- **All of the Old Testament history**
- **All of the fulfilled prophecies**

All of it was written to bring finally to Jesus Christ, the One who will save us from our sins.

Every sane man knows he is a sinner. He knows he is selfish, and he knows that he, and those like him, will use and abuse every opportunity they may have to be
- **Wealthy**
- **Comfortable and**

- **Powerful**

It's why the great philosophers wrestled with issues of morality and virtue.
How do we climb above our base inclinations?

It is also why the great leader of our world have fought for power and control.
How do we harness the power of the masses of people for our purpose?

It is why the great statesmen of our country strove to form "a more perfect union."
How do we build a government for the people and by the people?

But in every case, they were looking for a way to either
- **Harness the sin nature**
- **Restrain the sin nature or**
- **Reform the sin nature**

Only God promises to take away the sin nature.

And it is not through
- **Education**
- **Legislation or**
- **Diligence**
But by grace, through faith in the Lord, Jesus Christ.

We do not work our way to forgiveness of sin, we ask our way to that forgiveness.

Listen to this promise.
Romans 10:13 KJV
For whosoever shall call upon the name of the Lord shall be saved.

- **Not could be**
- **Not might be**

- **Not may be**

For whosoever shall call upon the name of the Lord shall be saved.

What a promise!

"But I have asked Christ to save me and I still sin." Hence comes promise number two and,

The Promise of
B. Chains broken
1 Corinthians 6:9-11 KJV
Know ye not that the unrighteous shall not inherit the kingdom of God? Be not deceived: neither fornicators, nor idolaters, nor adulterers, nor effeminate, nor abusers of themselves with mankind,
Nor thieves, nor covetous, nor drunkards, nor revilers, nor extortioners, shall inherit the kingdom of God.
And such were some of you: but ye are washed, but ye are sanctified, but ye are justified in the name of the Lord Jesus, and by the Spirit of our God.

Between these two we have the two most profound doctrines involving salvation
- **Justification** – God pronounces us innocent, free from sin
- **Sanctification** – God undertakes to wash us and break the chains of sin that bind us

Colossians 1:21-22 KJV
And you, that were sometime alienated and enemies in your mind by wicked works, yet now hath he reconciled
In the body of his flesh through death, to present you holy and unblameable and unreproveable in his sight:

God's promise is that He will present you to Himself
- **Holy**
- **Unblameable and**
- **Unreproveable**

in His sight.

Finally, there is…
The Promise of

C. Heaven waiting

John 14:1-3 KJV

Let not your heart be troubled: ye believe in God, believe also in me.
In my Father's house are many mansions: if it were not so, I would
have told you. I go to prepare a place for you.
And if I go and prepare a place for you, I will come again, and receive
you unto myself; that where I am, there ye may be also.

The day Jesus ascended into heaven, the disciples, stood
gazing into the sky, astounded at what had just taken place
when the Bible says,
Acts 1:10-11 KJV

…, behold, two men stood by them in white apparel;
Which also said, Ye men of Galilee, why stand ye gazing up into
heaven? this same Jesus, which is taken up from you into heaven, shall
so come in like manner as ye have seen him go into heaven.

And this promise of Jesus' return to receive us into heaven
with Him is our blessed hope,
Titus 2:13 KJV

Looking for that blessed hope, and the glorious appearing of the great
God and our Saviour Jesus Christ;

This Bible is the inspired Word of God. He spoke to men and
anointed them with the Holy Spirit to record for you and for
me the very Words God wanted you and me to hear from
Him.
- **It has proven itself to be His word**
- **It has changed the hearts of men who have believed it and**
- **It promises the saved an eternal home with Christ in heaven**

Chapter Eight

The History of the Bible
Hebrews 1:1-2

413 times the Bible tell us "*thus saith The Lord*" Phrases like, "*and God said*" fill the pages of our Bibles.

We know that the Bible us given by the inspiration of God. It is literally "**God breathed**." The question I want to address in this chapter, is, how did God breath it? In other words,

- **How were the men of God moved?**
- **How did God speak in those times passed?**

The answer is a picture of the grace of God, blending

- **The supernatural with the normal,**
- **The miraculous with the manly and**
- **The divine with the daily**

THE ORAL TRADITION
… prior to Moses

A. The oldest book of the Bible is the book of Job and is written in a style similar to a journal
But the earliest events,

- **Of Genesis**
- **Of the fall of Adam and Eve**
- **Of the flood and**
- **Of the call of Abraham from the Ur of Chaldees**
- **Of the growth of the Jewish nation**

Were all written by Moses almost 2500 hundred years after they happened.

B. How Moses came to know these things is a marvel in God's design

1. Remember that that the earliest men lived to be nearly one thousand years old

What that means is that the story of creation was only a little more than two generations old when the Jews went into Egypt.

The legal world accepts as authentic a witness who saw the originals or heard from the original. For instance, a man who knew George Washington would be considered an authoritative witness on the life of Washington. So a man who knew Adam would be an authoritative witness on the life of Adam. And Noah could have easily been personally acquainted with Adam or at a minimum, with His son, Seth.

The flood happened about 2500 BC.

2. We know that men in Mesopotamia could write at least by 3000 BC

Adam was created about 4000 BC. He lived long enough to have been able to write himself. Evolutionists teach that there was a time when men could not write. That's probably not true.

There was a society, called the Harappans[24], who lived in what is modern day Pakistan (not too far from the Garden of Eden) from about 3500 BC to 2500 BC (about the time of the Flood)[25]

- **They had a written language**
- **They had cities laid out with streets as wide as ours and blocks just as cities do today and**
- **They had indoor toilets with covered sewer systems**

---

[24] http://history-world.org/indus_valley.htm

[25] I am aware that there is no scientific evidence that the Harappan civilization was pre-flood. I merely present this as an evidence that ancient peoples were much more intelligent than we are sometimes led to believe. There is no reason to suppose they could not have kept a written record which was then passed down the next generation through the birthright blessing.

- **They have even discovered remains of people in Harappa with dental fillings[26]**

The Bible never does describe cave men type humans. Adam was created intelligent enough to name every animal on the earth. From him descended:
- **Musicians**
- **Workers with metal**
- **Workers with pottery**
- **City planners and undoubtedly**
- **People who could record what was going on around them**

In God's providence, the Jews went into Egypt where Moses was eventually born and, through a series of events that were not necessarily miraculous but were certainly *orchestrated of God*, Moses was raised in the home of the Pharaoh and educated in Egypt, the largest repository of written documents in that time.

3. Some experts[27] suggest that Moses would have had access to documents written by:
- **Adam**
- **Noah**
- **Shem, Ham and Japheth**
- **Terah (Abrahams father)**
- **Abraham**
- **Ishmael**
- **Esau**
- **Jacob and**
- **Joseph**

And even quoted from them as he recorded the story of the Genesis.

4. Jacob, as the possessor of the family's birthright blessing, would have kept those documents, and Joseph, as

---

[26] https://en.wikipedia.org/wiki/Indus_Valley_Civilization
[27] http://www.answersingenesis.org/articles/2011/06/28/did-moses-write-genesis

second in command of Egypt, would have had the ability to have them placed in the Egyptian library. Moses was led of the Lord to record, in a useable format, the Genesis. But that is not all he wrote.

THE WRITTEN WORD
of Moses and the Prophets
2 Peter 1:21 tells us
For the prophecy came not in old time by the will of man: but holy men of God spake as they were moved by the Holy Ghost.

Of course, Moses was moved of the Holy Ghost in his study of and recording the Genesis.

But beginning in Exodus through Deuteronomy,
A. Moses is a firsthand witness.
He, like John,[28] wrote what he
- **Saw**
- **Experienced and**
- **His own hands had handled**

B. We now get into the area of *special revelation*
Much of what we find in Moses and the prophets is their testimony of those things they witnessed. The hand of The Lord guided their record so
- **They gave an accurate record and**
- **They gave that part of the record that transmits the message God has for us**

Like John 20[29] much more could have been written, but what was written was written that we might know and believe.

---

[28] 1 John 1:1 KJV
That which was from the beginning, which we have heard, which we have seen with our eyes, which we have looked upon, and our hands have handled, of the Word of life;
[29] John 20:30-31 KJV
And many other signs truly did Jesus in the presence of his disciples, which are not written in this book:

C. But most of what we have in the Bible is much more than a record of history

It is a record of God speaking to the men who spoke to us. And God spake, *"in divers manners"* in different and miraculous ways.

To Moses:
- **In a burning bush**
- **The Ten Commandments with the finger of God**
- **Through manifestations of lightening and thunder on Sinai**

To the prophets:
- **He spoke to Joshua as a warrior with a sword**
- **He spoke to Gideon as the angel of The Lord**
- **He spoke with Samuel in an audible voice.**
- **He spoke to Daniel through dreams and**
- **He spoke to Isaiah and the other prophets through visions**

THE LIVING WORD

Jesus Christ
Hebrews 1:1-2

God, who at sundry times and in divers manners spake in time past unto the fathers by the prophets,
Hath in these last days spoken unto us by his Son, whom he hath appointed heir of all things, by whom also he made the worlds;

A. Now that was a truly SPECIAL REVELATION
- **That God spoke in a burning bush, is marvelous**
- **That God spoke with His voice to Samuel is awesome**
- **That God thundered His Word on Sinai is terrifying (in the sense of power)**

But that God became man and dwelt among us, is indeed gracious revelation.

But these are written, that ye might believe that Jesus is the Christ, the Son of God; and that believing ye might have life through his name.

I like to read. I do it all of the time. I learn almost everything I get to learn through the written word. But my favorite learning style is through the spoken word

- **Lectures**
- **Preaching**

I think that is partly why God called me to preach and why I love to preach so much.

- **It is my favorite way to learn so**
- **It is my favorite way to teach**

I say that to say,

- **I am glad for the Old Testament but**
- **I am amazed at the Gospels**

God became man and dwelt among us.

Everything Jesus said is the Word of God.

- **When He prays over a meal, it is the word of God**
- **When He encourages a sick child, it is the Word of God**
- **When He gives instructions to His disciples it is the word of God**

B. But Christ ascended into heaven long before what we have as the New Testament was finished

What about that? How do we get the rest of our New Testament? The answer is that the disciples finished the work of Christ.

Colossians 1:24

Who now rejoice in my sufferings for you, and fill up that which is behind of the afflictions of Christ in my flesh for his body's sake, which is the church:

Paul recognized that he was "[*filling]] up that which is* behind of the afflictions of Christ" in other words; that which Christ did not do while He was on the earth…

How in the world could he have done that?

Galatians 2:20
I am crucified with Christ: nevertheless I live; yet not I, but Christ liveth in me: and the life which I now live in the flesh I live by the faith of the Son of God, who loved me, and gave himself for me.

Christ was still present in the world through to the finish of the New Testament through the Apostles.

And He communicated through them by
1. The doctrine they taught
Acts 2:42
And they continued stedfastly in the apostles' doctrine and fellowship, and in breaking of bread, and in prayers.

The Apostles' doctrine would be useless doctrine with this one exception, their doctrine was given them by Jesus Christ.

Jesus communicated through them by
2. The letters they wrote
Colossians 4:16
And when this epistle is read among you, cause that it be read also in the church of the Laodiceans; and that ye likewise read the epistle from Laodicea.

Paul knew what he wrote was Scripture.

Peter also acknowledged that what Paul wrote was Scripture
2 Peter 3:15-16 KJV
And account that the longsuffering of our Lord is salvation; even as our beloved brother Paul also according to the wisdom given unto him hath written unto you;
As also in all his epistles, speaking in them of these things; in which are some things hard to be understood, which they that are unlearned and unstable wrest, as they do also the other scriptures, unto their own destruction.

We don't have a direct confirmation that the writings of the other books of the New Testament as Scriptures like we do of Paul, but we can expect that what is true of Paul's work is true of the others.

And then Jesus communicated through them by
3. The churches they planted
Ephesians 2:20
And are built upon the foundation of the apostles and prophets, Jesus Christ himself being the chief corner stone

Which gets us to the heart of where we are right now; we have two blessings, left to us by the Lord, each one intended to manifest the presence of God in our midst today:
- **Your Bible and**
- **Your local church**

Between the two of them you possess treasures of incalculable worth.

In the Bible God lays out for you his plans
- **To give you eternal life**
- **To restore your fellowship with Him and**
- **To prepare for you a place in heaven**

In the local church God unites His people together
- **To urge souls to be saved**
- **To provoke believers to love and good works and**
- **To remind His children of their blessed hope**

Chapter Nine

Could He? Would He? Did He?

Psalms 12:6-7 KJV

I recently finished watching a series of lectures on the History of the Peoples of the World by Professor Richard Bulliet of Columbia University. Bulliet is an acknowledged expert in history but says repeatedly throughout the series that historians are guessing about history.

The series of lectures uses a collegiate level textbook, co-written by Bulliet. The lectures turn out to be more of an expose on the mistakes made in the very book he helped to write. At one point in the series he begins to say, "The truth is…" but then stops himself and with a chuckle says, "…What do I know about truth!"

Here is a man then that acknowledges he does not know the truth. But very early on in the series he does establish as one unquestionable fact (at least in his mind and those of his students); the Bible is not true. He knows nothing about truth but guarantees his students that the Bible is not true.

I am here to proclaim to you that I know the Bible is true. Further. I know that the Bible I am preaching from today is completely true and has no error. I want to address a doctrine called the **preservation of Scripture.**

Every Christian I know would agree that God's Word was without mistakes when God originally gave it. But there are differences of opinion as to whether what we have in our hands this morning is still as perfect as it was in the beginning.

I want to approach the subject with three questions:

- Could God preserve His Words without error if He chose to do so?
- Would God have a reason to preserve His words to man without error? And finally
- Did God preserve His Word for us?

COULD GOD?

Job 42:1-2 KJV

Then Job answered the LORD, and said,
I know that thou canst do every thing, and that no thought can be withholden from thee.

Many years ago, while I was the Executive Vice President of Heartland Baptist Bible College, I prepared a message out of this passage. One of my best friends was Jamie Jett.
- He served as our Dean of Men at the time but
- He had also been a pastor for many years.

As I was preparing that message, Brother Jett came into my office and I began to talk to him about the text. I commented that one of my first observations when beginning to study the passage was that it says **God can do everything**, not **God can to anything**. And we began talking about the difference Brother Jett illustrated the difference by saying, "There is a huge difference between saying
- "Honey, I am going to the store. Do you want anything?" versus,
- "Honey, I am going to the store. Do you want everything?"

Job knew that God could do everything.
- He could speak and create the heavens and the earth
- He could will it and Flood the whole planet
- He could command it and the Red Sea would part
- He could choose it and the earth would open up
- He could promise and an enemy would be destroyed
- He could make the moon stand still
- He could make the sun turn backward
- He could raise a boy back to life
- He could stop the heart of a wicked enemy of David

In the New Testament
- **He could become man through the virgin, Mary**
- **He could turn water into wine**
- **He could heal servants, little girls and sick widows**
- **He could cast demons out of those living among the tombs**
- **He could raise Jairus' daughter, the boy at Nain and Lazarus fro the dead**
- **He could walk on water**
- **He could calm the storms of the sea**
- **He could feed thousands with just a few pieces of bread and fish**

In fact, it would be much easier to answer
- **What can't God do? than it would be to answer**
- **What can God do?**

"I know" Job said to God, *"Thou canst do everything..."*

So I may ask the question today:
Could God preserve the Bible word for word accurate and without error today?

A. If you were to read the positions of the prominent Bible publishers, you would think not.
Each new version of the Bible claims to be an improvement upon the version previous to it and since you can't improve on perfection the obvious conclusion is they do not believe the Bible versions before theirs were perfect. (Nor do they claim perfection for their own.)

B. If you were to hear the sermons of the famous television and radio evangelists of our day, you would think not
Every one of them reads from a different version of the Bible. Very often they make statements to the effect of, "A better translation would be..." Every time they do that they imply that they are better linguists than those who originally

translated the Bible into our language.

The fact is, almost no preacher in America today is a linguist at all – they are all merely aping the words of someone they read – who probably was no linguist himself.

C. If you are not careful, the very notes and hints that you find in your Bible would lead you to believe God could not preserve His Word
Phrases such as, "Older and more reliable manuscripts omit this verse." Abound in the footnotes of many of the Bibles we can purchase these days.

But we still face the question; *"Could God preserve His Bible perfect and without mistakes today?"*

I am no linguist, but I am
- **A child of God**
- **A preacher of righteousness and**
- **A follower of Jesus Christ**

And I insist to you, if God is God at all He can.
- **If He can call into existence the heavens and the earth, He can preserve His word without mistakes**
- **If He can part the Red Sea, He can preserve His Word without mistakes**
- **If He can dwell among us as Jesus did, He can preserve His Word without mistakes**

Could God preserve His Word without mistakes?

The answer is a resounding, of course He could.

WOULD GOD?
Would it be the will of God to preserve His Bible perfect and without mistakes today?

God can do anything He wills to do. The question then is, **Did God want to preserve His Word perfectly?**

The Bible makes it very clear that God had no intention to allow man to mess up His Bible. He gave it to us as His communication to man how to be forgiven of our sin and given a home in heaven.

The message is just too important to let it be corrupted by the errors of man.

A. Let's look at some Bible:
Psalms 12:6-7 KJV
The words of the LORD are pure words: as silver tried in a furnace of earth, purified seven times.
Thou shalt keep them, O LORD, thou shalt preserve them from this generation for ever.

To be fair, I should point out that those who do not believe God has preserved His Word perfectly do not believe this verse is a promise to preserve His Word the Bible. They see it as meaning that God will keep His promise to protect His people from their enemies. In other words, God promises to protect his people and God here promises his promise is pure.

I don't have a problem with that interpretation. I only have a problem with limiting it to one generation and one people.

The Bible as a whole is a promise to protect His people from their enemies
- **The world**
- **The flesh and**
- **The Devil**

The Bible as a whole is a promise to
- **Bring lost souls to an awareness of their sin**
- **Point those same souls to Jesus, the One who will take away their sin and**
- **Rescue those who come to Christ from their sin and its**

punishment in eternal hell
Psalms 12:6-7 is God's promise that His promise is pure and will remain pure forever.

By the way, notice the passage promises to preserve His "words" and not just His Word. The modernist argues that while all versions of the Bible today have some mistakes, the gist of the Word is still trustworthy and accurate.
- **They would say that we can trust God's Word**
- **Even if we can't trust His words**

I am telling you that you can trust every Word of the Bible, even if you don't yet understand why God has preserved a particular Word in the Bible.

B. This isn't the only passage that expresses God's willingness to preserve His Words
Matthew 5:17-18 KJV
Think not that I am come to destroy the law, or the prophets: I am not come to destroy, but to fulfil.
For verily I say unto you, Till heaven and earth pass, one jot or one tittle shall in no wise pass from the law, till all be fulfilled.

Notice a few things here.
1. God's willingness to preserve His Word
The law and the prophets is a term describing the Bible.

Jesus said He did not come to destroy it but to fulfill it. The will of Jesus is to fulfill the Word of God, not to see it destroyed or compromised in any way.

2. His will is that every jot and tittle be fulfilled and not merely the gist of the Bible
The jot and tittle would be small pieces of grammar like our dotting the "I" and crossing the "T". It is another indication that God words are preserved and not merely the Word. I may not yet understand why everything in the Bible is there just as it is. If I understood all of God's Word, it wouldn't be

much of a divine book. But I believe that God is **capable of** and **willing to** preserve every piece of His Bible right down to the smallest word …forever.

Would God preserve His Word without mistakes? The answer again is a resounding, of course He would.

DID GOD?
Since God can and God would preserve His Bible perfect and without mistakes, it is only right to ask the question, *"Did he do it?"*

This question, in my opinion, is the pivot point between
- **Those who believe, as I do, that we have a preserved Bible and**
- **Those who believe, as the majority of modern "scholars", that there are mistakes in the Bible we have today.**

No believer to my knowledge argues that **God's Word was imperfect in its original form.** Nor do they argue that **God could have kept it perfect had He chosen to do so.**

I would like for you to see that the earliest Christians believed that God had preserved His Words without error.

A. Paul believed that God had preserved His Words perfectly
2 Timothy 3:15-17 KJV
And that from a child thou hast known the holy scriptures, which are able to make thee wise unto salvation through faith which is in Christ Jesus.
All scripture is given by inspiration of God, and is profitable for doctrine, for reproof, for correction, for instruction in righteousness:
That the man of God may be perfect, throughly furnished unto all good works.

Notice that he says "all scripture"
- **Not just parts of it**

- **Not just the gist of it**
- **Not major message of it**

He said that all scripture is given by inspiration and that it is all profitable. If it is all profitable, it must all be infallible and without mistakes.

B. Peter believed that God had preserved His Words perfectly

1 Peter 1:23-25 KJV

Being born again, not of corruptible seed, but of incorruptible, by the word of God, which liveth and abideth for ever.
For all flesh is as grass, and all the glory of man as the flower of grass. The grass withereth, and the flower thereof falleth away:
But the word of the Lord endureth for ever. And this is the word which by the gospel is preached unto you.

Two phrases give us Peter's understanding of the preservation of the Bible:

1. He says it is incorruptible

I am not sure how to interpret that unless that means, without error mistakes or the possibility of containing error and mistakes

The word corruption is used in Peter's Pentecostal message to contrast the dead bodies of David and Jesus

- **David's body stayed dead and corrupted**
- **Jesus' body resurrected and did not corrupt**

That is how we ought to view the Bible.

- **It is alive**
- **It is vital and**
- **It has never been corrupted**

That is not to say it has never been attacked. There are any number of versions of the Bible that are corrupted. But God has seen to it that there has also always been a Bible that is without corruption.

2. He says, *"the Word of the Lord endureth forever."*
Once again, I do not know how to understand this phrase unless it means that God's Word survives withering and falling away.

Conclusion
One of the silliest things I think Satan ever introduced into the world is the idea that:

- **God spoke to people His living Word**
- **God led them to record that living Word in written form but then**
- **God allowed mistakes to be introduced into His Word**

so that we cannot be sure what we have today is the perfect Word of God. If I have no assurance that God preserved His Words perfectly then I have no real way to know what His Word for me may be and what might be the result of human or Satanic corruption. And, don't you see, that removes all authority from the Bible. It gives me the right to pick and choose which parts I like and want to obey and which parts I do not

I am convinced that:

- **God could preserve His Word without mistakes**
- **God would want to preserve His Word without mistakes and**
- **God did preserve His Word without mistakes**

in the King James Version of the Bible.

Chapter Ten
The Message of the Bible
Hebrews 1:1-2 KJV

One of the most basic studies in the Academic world is that of Homer's *Iliad* and *Odyssey.*

The *Iliad* is set in the Trojan War between the Greeks and Trojans, which, the story says started when the Trojan Prince, Paris, stole Helen, the Wife of the Greek Prince, Menelaus. The Greeks cross the ocean and slaughter the Trojans. The things they do in war disturb even the Greeks. They are shocked at their own barbarism.

The *Odyssey* is the sequel. The war is over, and the heroes are returning home. But the journey home is not quick and their experiences in their travels are meant to atone for their barbary as well and teach them lessons about why they are like they are.

These two epics were written about the same time as Isaiah, and are supposedly set in a period of time, about the same as the Jew's exodus from Egypt. The earliest colleges considered the study of Homer's epics as fundamental to education. They are still foundational to secular studies in the humanities.

Secular scholarship views them as a sort of Bible. And their comparison is not that far off:
- **Both the Bible and the Epics deal with man's relationship to God (or gods)**
- **Both the Bible and the Epics deal with man at war with men**
- **Both the Bible and Epics seeks to address the struggles men have with their (sin) nature**

- **Both the Bible and the Epics claim divine inspiration**[30]

But rather than seeing a comparison between the two, I see a contrast. Homer's Epic, *The Odyssey*, begins with the word "**Man**." The lecturer I was listening to then commented that "Man is the central theme of the Epic, and thus, of the Greek's search for truth."[31]

The lost world
- **Begins with man,**
- **Focuses on man and**
- **Learns what he can of man**

through meditations and explorations about man. This is in direct contrast with the Bible which begins with "God".

Genesis 1:1 KJV
In the beginning God created the heaven and the earth.

God, not man, is the central theme of the Bible.

Christians,
- **Begin with God**
- **Focus on God and**
- **Learn what we do of man**

through our meditations and explorations, not of man, but of God.

The Bible

---

[30] Homer's concept of inspiration was definitely different than that of the prophets, but he nonetheless did claim to be the spokesperson for the muse. He believed the deity would move him and use him as it wills.

[31] "The first word, in Homer's Epic, is the Greek word andra, which indeed means man.

…As the first word in the epic, in the Greek this tells us what the epic is all about.

It is epic that, that first word indicates that whole and most important theme of the story." (Peter Struck, University of Pennsylvania, Greek and Roman Mythology, Coursera, 2013)

- **Begins with man's broken fellowship with God as the reason we are capable of such disturbing things**
- **Chronicles the result of our sin nature and**
- **Offers us a means of atonement and restored fellowship**

In every page of the Bible we are reminded that we are sinful beings but in every page of the Bible we are also offered hope of a sinless future

The Bible is God's message to man, and it gives to us three main lessons:

THAT GOD IS HOLY

Isaiah 6:1-3 KJV

In the year that king Uzziah died I saw also the Lord sitting upon a throne, high and lifted up, and his train filled the temple.
Above it stood the seraphims: each one had six wings; with twain he covered his face, and with twain he covered his feet, and with twain he did fly.
And one cried unto another, and said, Holy, holy, holy, is the LORD of hosts: the whole earth is full of his glory.

The word **holy** means
- **Clean**
- **Pure**
- **Dedicated**

It means more than that God is without sin. It even means more than that God must keep separate from sin. It means that God is the defining point of what is sin and what is not.

- **Anything like God is not sin**
- **Anything unlike God is sin**

As the Creator of all things, He is the plumb line, the measure. God is the standard for everything that is right and wrong.

This is a huge question. Men have been debating it for years; who gets to decide what is right and wrong, moral and immoral?

Is it the wealthy?
If you have enough money to buy your friend and bribe your enemies do you get to pick good and evil?

Is it the powerful?
Do you get to pick right and wrong when you have the power to make men do as you please?

Is it the majority?
Does murder become right when enough people don't think it is wrong?
Can governments *by the people* and *for the people* legislate *to the people* their morality?

The message of the Bible is very clear.
Morality is from God.

He alone is holy
- **The standard**
- **The measure**
- **The plumb line**

He is the separating line between what is good and what is evil.

God says
Isaiah 55:9 KJV
For as the heavens are higher than the earth, so are my ways higher than your ways, and my thoughts than your thoughts.

Revelation 15:3 KJV says
And they sing the song of Moses the servant of God, and the song of the Lamb, saying, Great and marvellous are thy works, Lord God Almighty; just and true are thy ways, thou King of saints.

God's
- **Ways and**
- **Works and**
- **Thoughts**

Are
- **Marvelous and**
- **Just and**
- **True**

- **God's creation of Adam and Eve was right**
- **God's restriction from the tree of the knowledge of good and evil was right**
- **God's judgment when they ate of that fruit was right**

Further
- **God's determination that a Saviour would be from Abraham was right**
- **God's design to focus His attention on the Jews was right**
- **God's deliverance through only one Saviour is right**

- **What God says about life and death is right**
- **What God says about obedience and disobedience is right**
- **What God says about marriage is right**
- **What God says about faith and religion is right**

It doesn't matter if we agree or disagree.
- **He is the standard**
- **He is the measure**
- **He is the plumb line**

God is holy and everything is settled upon Him

THAT MAN HAS SINNED

Romans 3:23 KJV
For all have sinned, and come short of the glory of God;

We tend to make light of our sin.
- **We don't see it as all that bad.**

- As long as we aren't hurting anybody else, we think we are free to do as we please.

We also tend to measure sin in relative terms
- My sins are petty, hardly worth thinking about
- Some sins are terrible, and we ought to have rules against them
- Very few sins are deplorable, disturbing, they ought to be stopped at all costs

That is not the message about sin we find in the Bible. In this book we discover that our sins are
- Inherited from Adam and Eve
- Inhabited in our nature and
- Exhibited in our actions

A. Inherited from Adam and Eve
Romans 5:12-14 KJV
Wherefore, as by one man sin entered into the world, and death by sin; and so death passed upon all men, for that all have sinned:
(For until the law sin was in the world: but sin is not imputed when there is no law.
Nevertheless death reigned from Adam to Moses, even over them that had not sinned after the similitude of Adam's transgression, who is the figure of him that was to come.

We all know what an inheritance is. Our father possesses something and when he passes away, he gives it to us. Because of their sin, Adam and Eve possessed death and separation from God. And they have been passing on that possession to their children ever since.

King David wrote,
Psalms 51:5 KJV
Behold, I was shapen in iniquity; and in sin did my mother conceive me.

I am separated from God at my birth. If it were possible to live without ever sinning, I would still be separated from God and die because I have inherited it from Adam and Eve.

Furthermore, sin is
B. Inhabited in our nature
Romans 3:13-18 KJV

Their throat is an open sepulchre; with their tongues they have used deceit; the poison of asps is under their lips:
Whose mouth is full of cursing and bitterness:
Their feet are swift to shed blood:
Destruction and misery are in their ways:
And the way of peace have they not known:
There is no fear of God before their eyes.

This is heaven's autopsy of the man who is dead in trespasses and sins. God's CSI cuts open the sinner and discovers that from the foot to the face, every one of us is completely filled with sin. The Greeks could do the disturbing things they did at Troy because they were filled face to feet with sin.

And so are you.
- **It may be that your sin nature has been restrained through discipline**
- **It may be that you have been able to keep it, for the most part under lock and key**

But it still exists in you.

George Washington was, in his own lifetime, considered one of the most virtuous men alive. His reputation of virtue was a purposeful one. As a young man Washington had memorized a set of rules of manners and behavior and forced himself to practice those rules. He was a disciplined man and it paid off in his reputation.

At the end of the American Revolution, Washington did what no one in history had done before him.

- **Commanding an army that had just defeated the most powerful army in the world and**
- **Dwelling in a land that was freshly without any king or government to lead it**
- **Capable at that moment to take over the country for himself**

George Washington resigned as Commander in Chief of that army. When news of his resignation reached King George in England he is said to have remarked, "Then truly, Washington is the greatest man alive."

But Washington had a sin nature. Though he kept in under control most of the time, he had a terrible temper and it was unleashed from time to time. Once when he was President, he was meeting with his cabinet, including John Adams, Alexander Hamilton and John Adams. An aide entered the room and showed Washington a political cartoon of him that was not very kind. Jefferson later wrote about the incident and said that Washington blew up in a rage, yelling and screaming and throwing things

- **He said he had never wanted to be President**
- **He said he did not want to be President and**
- **He said he hated those cartoons picking on him**

Once his outburst was over, the room became quiet and they had to dismiss the meeting. It was impossible to work in the atmosphere Washington's unleashed temper had created.

I offer that as an illustration of what is in all of us. You may have bridled your sin nature well enough that

- **You aren't in jail and**
- **Most people like you**

But it still exists in you.

So that our sin is
C. Exhibited in our actions
Romans 3:10-12 KJV
As it is written, There is none righteous, no, not one:
There is none that understandeth, there is none that seeketh after God.

They are all gone out of the way, they are together become unprofitable;

There is none of us that do good. And even the seeming "good" that we do is always done for motives that are less than good.

This sets up a conflict between *God, who is holy* and *man, who is sinful.*

Romans 8:7 KJV
Because the carnal mind is enmity against God: for it is not subject to the law of God, neither indeed can be.

Romans 8:7 not only tells us that this enmity exists, but that it is impossible for men to reverse it.

- **The mind of the sinner is not subject to the law of God and further**
- **The mind of the sinner can't be subject to the law of God**

This brings us to – *the Good News*
THAT THERE IS A RECONCILER
Ephesians 2:13-16 KJV
But now in Christ Jesus ye who sometimes were far off are made nigh by the blood of Christ.
For he is our peace, who hath made both one, and hath broken down the middle wall of partition between us;
Having abolished in his flesh the enmity, even the law of commandments contained in ordinances; for to make in himself of twain one new man, so making peace;
And that he might reconcile both unto God in one body by the cross, having slain the enmity thereby:

Colossians 1:21-22 KJV says
And you, that were sometime alienated and enemies in your mind by wicked works, yet now hath he reconciled
In the body of his flesh through death, to present you holy and unblameable and unreproveable in his sight:

- **What I cannot do because of my sin nature**
- **What religion cannot do because it was not designed to do it**

God Himself did, by becoming a man and making those who come to Him, new men.

This good news
- **That God became a man**
- **That God died for our sins and**
- **That God saves whosoever will call upon His name**

A. Is promised throughout the Old Testament
Genesis 3:14-15 KJV
And the LORD God said unto the serpent, Because thou hast done this, thou art cursed above all cattle, and above every beast of the field; upon thy belly shalt thou go, and dust shalt thou eat all the days of thy life:
And I will put enmity between thee and the woman, and between thy seed and her seed; it shall bruise thy head, and thou shalt bruise his heel.

Genesis 3:15 is just the first of a long list of Old Testament promises extending for here
- **To Abraham**
- **To Isaac**
- **To Jacob**
- **To Judah**
- **To David**
- **To Bethlehem-Epratah**

- **David**
- **Daniel**
- **Isaiah and**
- **Malachi**

are just a few among the many writers of the Old Testament who all point our attention to the promised Saviour.

- **Every sacrifice the Jews offered**
- **Every feast they observed**
- **Every event that was a part of their culture**

was designed to point their attention to the promised Saviour. Even their failure to keep the whole law was meant as a schoolmaster to bring them to Christ.[32]

B. Is perfected in the Gospels
Matthew 1:18-21 KJV
Now the birth of Jesus Christ was on this wise: When as his mother Mary was espoused to Joseph, before they came together, she was found with child of the Holy Ghost.
Then Joseph her husband, being a just man, and not willing to make her a publick example, was minded to put her away privily.
But while he thought on these things, behold, the angel of the Lord appeared unto him in a dream, saying, Joseph, thou son of David, fear not to take unto thee Mary thy wife: for that which is conceived in her is of the Holy Ghost.
And she shall bring forth a son, and thou shalt call his name JESUS: for he shall save his people from their sins.

All that God had promised was fulfilled with the
- **Miraculous Incarnation**
- **Sinless Inhabitation**
- **Vicarious Crucifixion and**
- **Glorious Resurrection**

of Jesus Christ

The promise of the good news
C. Is presented through the rest of the New Testament
Acts 1:1-2 KJV
The former treatise have I made, O Theophilus, of all that Jesus began both to do and teach,
Until the day in which he was taken up, after that he through the Holy Ghost had given commandments unto the apostles whom he had chosen:

Everything we find in the Bible after the resurrection and ascension of Christ into heaven is

---

[32] Galatians 3:24 KJV
Wherefore the law was our schoolmaster to bring us unto Christ, that we might be justified by faith.

- **A demonstration of the power of the gospel to change lives and**
- **An instruction to the people of God how to put this new life to use**

Ephesians 2:10 KJV
For we are his workmanship, created in Christ Jesus unto good works, which God hath before ordained that we should walk in them.

God didn't save us so we could sit back and revel in our victory but to pick up our tools and put our hands to work in His name.

Chapter Eleven

The Power of the Bible
Romans 1:13-16 KJV

I was crossing Snoqualmie Pass recently, as construction crews were preparing for rock blasting work that evening, my grandson, Joshua, started asking questions about what rock blasting was. His dad said that the crews would drill a hole in the rock and put the dynamite in the hole. Then, when the dynamite blew up, it would make a big hole in the rocks. Joshua asked if we could stay and watch them do the blasting. His dad said, "No, I don't think they will let you watch." Joshua said, "Ok Daddy, when I grow up, I want to learn about that because I am curious."

I can't imagine a man who isn't curious about
- **Explosions**
- **Blasting and**
- **Dynamite**

It's built into the DNA of men to gravitate toward power:
- **Large engines**
- **Power tools**
- **Big caliber guns**
- **Chain saws and**
- **Dynamite**

Nearly every male in this room has, at some point in their lives, foolishly experimented with explosions. We like dynamite.

I want to remind you that, if you are holding a Bible right now, you are holding dynamite in your hands.
Romans 1:16 says,
… I am not ashamed of the gospel of Christ: for it is the power of God unto salvation to every one that believeth; to the Jew first, and also to the Greek.

The word power in this passage comes from the Greek Word that means dynamite. The Bible has proven itself to be dynamite since the first pages were written more than four thousand years ago.

- **Many people have foolishly ignored the power of the Bible but**
- **Many others have been radically changed, transformed by the message it brings.**

The Bible is
- **So much more than a religious book**
- **So much more than spiritual theories**
- **So much more than the history of a particular group of religious people**

The Bible is power.

I want to give to you five things the Bible you hold in your hands has power to do:

POWER TO SAVE
Romans 1:16
... I am not ashamed of the gospel of Christ: for it is the power of God unto salvation to every one that believeth; to the Jew first, and also to the Greek.

The word saved has some religious baggage attached to it these days, but I still think it is the right word to use to express to people what God offers us.

A. Saved expresses deliverance
To be saved from something means that there is something dangerous we need to be rescued from.

Read in the pages of history and you will find that people of every century and everywhere in the world have known that that has to be some sort of judgment for the despicable way that we are.

- We know we are abusive to others
- We know we are selfish
- We know we are jealous
- We know we are hot headed
- We know we are sinners

- We know there has to be some price to be paid for our sin and
- We know that judgment to be death and hell

Salvation is the word that describes our rescue from that judgment.

B. Saved expresses helplessness
If I need to be saved, it means that it is not something I can do for myself.

- I need a Saviour
- I need a rescuer
- I need someone to come do for me what I cannot do for myself

The salvation God offers is not a self help plan. I don't find in the Bible a series of do's and don'ts that, if I work them just right, will get me out of the fix I am in. My situation is worse than that. It's worse than just if I can get some things turned around in my life everything will turn out fine.

So,
- The Bible isn't a guide for living
- The Bible isn't a road map for life

The Bible is the sound of the evacuation helicopter[33] coming in with guns blazing at the enemy and at great expense to the

---

[33] On May 2, 1968, a 12-man Special Forces team was surrounded by a NVA battalion. Benavidez heard the radio appeal for help and boarded a helicopter to respond. Armed only with a knife, he jumped from the helicopter carrying a medical bag and rushed to join the trapped team.

Benavidez "distinguished himself by a series of daring and extremely glorious actions ... [*Realizing that all the team members were either dead or wounded and unable to move to the pickup zone, he directed the aircraft to a nearby clearing where he jumped from the hovering helicopter, and ran approximately 75 meters under withering small arms fire to the crippled team. Prior to reaching the team's position he was wounded in his right leg, face, and head. Despite these painful injuries, he took charge, repositioning the team members and directing their fire to facilitate the landing of an extraction aircraft, and the loading of wounded and dead team members. He then threw smoke canisters to direct the aircraft to the team's position. Despite his severe wounds and under intense enemy fire, he carried and dragged half of the wounded team members to the awaiting aircraft. He then provided protective fire by running alongside the aircraft as it moved to pick up the remaining team members. As the enemy's fire intensified, he hurried to recover the body and classified documents on the dead team leader. When he reached the leader's body, Sergeant Benavidez was severely wounded by small arms fire in the abdomen and grenade fragments in his back. At nearly the same moment, the aircraft pilot was mortally wounded, and his helicopter crashed. Although in extremely critical condition due to his multiple wounds, Sergeant Benavidez secured the classified documents and made his way back to the wreckage, where he aided the wounded out of the overturned aircraft, and gathered the stunned survivors into a defensive perimeter. Under increasing enemy automatic weapons and grenade fire, he moved around the perimeter distributing water and ammunition to his weary men, reinstilling in them a will to live and fight. Facing a buildup of enemy opposition with a beleaguered team, Sergeant Benavidez mustered his strength, began calling in tactical air strikes and directed the fire from supporting gunships to suppress the enemy's fire and so permit another extraction attempt. He was wounded again in his thigh by small arms fire while administering first aid to a wounded team member just before another extraction helicopter was able to land. His indomitable spirit kept him going as he began to ferry his comrades to the craft. On his second trip with the wounded, he was clubbed from behind by an enemy soldier. In the ensuing hand-to-hand combat, he sustained additional wounds to his head and arms before killing his adversary.*[3][note 1] He then continued under devastating fire to carry the wounded to the helicopter. Upon reaching the aircraft, he spotted and killed two enemy soldiers who were rushing the craft from an angle that prevented the aircraft door gunner from firing upon them. With little strength remaining, he made one last trip to the perimeter to ensure that all classified material had been collected or destroyed, and to bring in the remaining wounded. Only then, in extremely serious*

Saviour, taking the bullets that were meant for us and getting us out of harms way.

C. Saved expresses happiness
When a person is in that much danger and is that helpless to get out of trouble, when they are saved, they are happy about it.

The Bible is the power of God unto salvation.

POWER TO CLEANSE (sanctify)
Ephesians 5:25-27 KJV
Husbands, love your wives, even as Christ also loved the church, and gave himself for it;
That he might sanctify <u>and cleanse it with the washing of water by the word,</u>
That he might present it to himself a glorious church, not having spot, or wrinkle, or any such thing; but that it should be holy and without blemish.

Can you imagine how cheap and useless being saved would feel if all God did was to,
- **Forgive us of our sins**
- **Forget them to never be remembered again**

---

condition from numerous wounds and loss of blood, did he allow himself to be pulled into the extraction aircraft] ... and because of his gallant choice to join voluntarily his comrades who were in critical straits, to expose himself constantly to withering enemy fire, and his refusal to be stopped despite numerous severe wounds, saved the lives of at least eight men." He was believed dead after finally being evacuated and was being zipped up in a body bag when he mustered the last of his strength and spit in the face of a medic, thereby alerting nearby medical personnel that he was still alive. (see medal citation below)
Nearly dead from a total of 37 separate <u>bayonet</u>, bullet and shrapnel wounds received on multiple occasions over the course of the six hour fight between the 13 men and an enemy battalion, Benavidez was evacuated once again to Brooke Army Medical Center, where he eventually recovered. (https://en.wikipedia.org/wiki/Roy_Benavidez, accessed 5-3-13)

- **Promise us that we will get to live in heaven**

and then just leave us to try to deal with the truth that we still sin?

I consider God's work of changing me into the image of Christ one of the most wonderful parts of being a Christian.
- **It isn't always easy**
- **It very often hurts**

But I am glad that the Word of God has the power to save me and then to cleanse me that he might present me before the Lord without spot or wrinkle or any blemish of sin.

POWER TO DISCERN

Hebrews 4:12 KJV

For the word of God is quick, and powerful, and sharper than any twoedged sword, piercing even to the dividing asunder of soul and spirit, and of the joints and marrow, and is a discerner of the thoughts and intents of the heart.

The Bible says,

Jeremiah 17:9 KJV

The heart is deceitful above all things, and desperately wicked: who can know it?

The person we most easily deceive is ourselves.
- **We make light of our own sin**
- **We tend to build up our own egos**

Even when we have a poor self image, we can't see that even that is a form of self deception. How can we possibly grow as Christians, as parents, as human beings in general if we can't trust our hearts to tell us the truths about ourselves?

That's where the Bible comes in. It serves as a mirror, reflecting back to us the true nature of our beings.
- **We may not be faithful at looking into the mirror of God's Word**
- **We may not like what we see in the mirror**

But we can't help but see ourselves truthfully whenever we take a serious look into the Bible.

- **Jacob, wanting something so badly he will trick his brother to get it**
- **Moses, serving God so faithfully, but in a moment of anger ruining his testimony**
- **David, a good leader but a bad father**

Read the Bible carefully and we will see ourselves in every page. And it will cut to the quick and reveal what needs to change in us.

POWER TO CONVICT

1 Corinthians 1:18-24 KJV

For the preaching of the cross is to them that perish foolishness; but unto us which are saved it is the power of God.
For it is written, I will destroy the wisdom of the wise, and will bring to nothing the understanding of the prudent.
Where is the wise? where is the scribe? where is the disputer of this world? hath not God made foolish the wisdom of this world?
For after that in the wisdom of God the world by wisdom knew not God, it pleased God by the foolishness of preaching to save them that believe.
For the Jews require a sign, and the Greeks seek after wisdom:
But we preach Christ crucified, unto the Jews a stumblingblock, and unto the Greeks foolishness;
But unto them which are called, both Jews and Greeks, Christ the power of God, and the wisdom of God.

- **Those who are not Christians may despise the message of the Bible**
- **Those who are Christians may sometimes shrink back from the message of the Bible**

But this book will bring conviction to those who come under the sound of its preaching.

That's good news because we can never be cleansed unless we get under conviction.
1 John 1:9 KJV

If we confess our sins, he is faithful and just to forgive us our sins, and to cleanse us from all unrighteousness.

I believe this verse to be unquestionably true. If we come to God and confess to Him our sins, *"HE IS faithful and just to forgive us our sins and to cleanse us from all unrighteousness."*

But can you imagine coming to God and saying something like, "God, you said that I sin. You said if I confess my sins you will forgive them. I don't know of any sin I committed but if I did commit one today please forgive me." Do you think that has any hope of being answered by the Lord?

What about, "Lord, today I did this sin.
- **I like doing it**
- **I plan to keep doing it**
- **I don't see anything wrong with it**

But I want you to forgive me for it."

Is that going to get the promise of 1 John 1:9? Not on your life. The whole concept of confession carries with it contrition. Contrition comes from conviction. I must be convicted of my sin before I can repent of the sin. And only when I confess my sin (with that sort of repentance) can I hope to receive the promise that *"He is faithful and just to forgive us our sin and to cleanse us from all unrighteousness."*

POWER TO FEED (growth)
Luke 4:1-4 KJV
And Jesus being full of the Holy Ghost returned from Jordan, and was led by the Spirit into the wilderness,
Being forty days tempted of the devil. And in those days he did eat nothing: and when they were ended, he afterward hungered.
And the devil said unto him, If thou be the Son of God, command this stone that it be made bread.
And Jesus answered him, saying, It is written, That man shall not live by bread alone, but by every word of God.

Just before going to Jerusalem for his last time, the Apostle Paul called for the pastors of the churches in and around Ephesus. These are, he believes, his last instructions for them. The Holy Spirit has warned him that he will be captured put in prison and eventually die after arriving in Jerusalem.

Among his instructions for them he said,
Acts 20:28 KJV
Take heed therefore unto yourselves, and to all the flock, over the which the Holy Ghost hath made you overseers, to feed the church of God, which he hath purchased with his own blood.

Feed the church of God….
- **We don't do that by giving them bread and meet**
- **We don't do that my fixing them rice and beans**
- **We don't do that by opening a soup kitchen**

We feed the church of God "every Word of God."

I understand that we all need to eat. I also understand that from a practical point of view that food we need is material, not spiritual. But I have to tell you, the most important thing any of us needs is not food for the body but food for the soul. I may enjoy a good meal and it will keep me alive a few days. But the food God gives my soul lasts eternally.

- **The Bible is satisfying – I never read it without enjoying it**
- **The Bible is living – It says something new to me every day**
- **The Bible is sustaining – It solves the dilemma's I face in life**
- **The Bible is fulfilling – It has something for every interest**

I know that some Christians go without reading the Bible for long periods of time. I have learned that I need its nutrition far to much to go a day without it.

Fundamentals Concerning Eternity

Chapter Twelve
Fundamental Questions
Job 1:1-22 KJV
Job 2:1-10 KJV

The book of Job is one of the oldest pieces of ancient writings in existence.

Epic of Gilgamesh written about 1800 BC
Job written about or before 1500 BC
Homer's Odyssey written about 700 BC (but about tales dating back to 1500 BC)[34]

Consider the enormous difference in content:
While Odysseus is said to be traveling around the Mediterranean fighting one eyed monsters and visiting dead souls in the underworld – by feeding them cow's blood;
Job is wrestling with real world issues:
- **The death of his children**
- **The destruction of his property by a storm**
- **The discussions with his neighbors about issues of right and wrong**

There is a hint at Biblical preservation right here as well.
The Epic of Gilgamesh was written at about the same time and from about the same part of the world as was Job. Yet only a handful of fragments of the Epic exist today, while there are so many ancient pieces of the book of Job in existence that we do not have to wonder what was written.

The Epic of Gilgamesh has huge sections that have been filled in by scholars giving us their best guess what might

---

[34] Even Confucius and Buddha were 1000 years after the writing of Job.

have been written, other missing portions are so substantial that there is no guess possible. No one has to guess what the book of Job says. God has seen to it that we have more than sufficient copies to trust that this is exactly what the book of Job said in the original copy.

Job deals with real world issues. I am going to call them fundamental questions of life. This is just about the oldest existing human document. [35] And it is asking the same questions that we ask even today.

WHY THE SUFFERING?
Job 3:1-11 KJV

After this opened Job his mouth, and cursed his day.
And Job spake, and said,
Let the day perish wherein I was born, and the night in which it was said, There is a man child conceived.
Let that day be darkness; let not God regard it from above, neither let the light shine upon it.
Let darkness and the shadow of death stain it; let a cloud dwell upon it; let the blackness of the day terrify it.
As for that night, let darkness seize upon it; let it not be joined unto the days of the year, let it not come into the number of the months.
Lo, let that night be solitary, let no joyful voice come therein.
Let them curse it that curse the day, who are ready to raise up their mourning.
Let the stars of the twilight thereof be dark; let it look for light, but have none; neither let it see the dawning of the day:
Because it shut not up the doors of my mother's womb, nor hid sorrow from mine eyes.
Why died I not from the womb? why did I not give up the ghost when I came out of the belly?

Everything we know about Job tells us that the man should not have had to suffer as badly as he did in life:

- **He was a good man**

---

[35]Genesis covers things that happened before Job but was written by Moses several hundred years after Job's death.

- He was a generous man
- He was a godly man

And yet Job suffered
Emotionally – with the loss of his children
Financially – with the loss of his herds
Physically – with the loss of his health

Now here is a fact – every man who has ever lived has suffered in one way or another.
- **The poor suffer from poverty related difficulties**
- **The wealthy suffer from stress related difficulties**

Don't you find it ironic that Americans send money to help those who are dying of starvation in third world countries, while Americans are dying in even higher numbers from illnesses directly related to having too much to eat?

- **Those in the working classes suffer at the hands of oppressive leadership**
- **Those in leadership suffer from the pressures of high power rule**

An interesting study done frequently with the Presidents of the United States is to demonstrate how quickly they age while in office. Pictures of recent presidents when they enter office contrasted with pictures when they finish their office are striking. Young, healthy dark headed men enter the White House. Older, wrinkled gray headed men leave
- **They have the best of doctors**
- **They have access to the best foods**
- **They generally exercise every day**
But they turn old from the pressure of the office.

By the way, this must not be a brand-new phenomenon. During a stressful time in the history of our country, George Washington went to address an assembly of former Officers in his army who were upset over that their pensions had not been paid and were threatening a coup against the new government. Washington arrived and, as he prepared to speak, reached for his glasses in his coat pocket and, as he put them on said, "Excuse me gentlemen but, I have not only grown gray, but blind in the service of my country."[36]

So, Job, probably the oldest human document in existence today, with one of the most fundamental of all questions –

Why do people suffer so?

No doubt you have asked that very same question.
- **Maybe it was during a time when you were really suffering**
- **Maybe it was while watching someone you love suffer badly**
- **Maybe it's happening right now**

By the way, the book of Job does not answer the question. There are sixty-five more books of the Bible that serve to do that.

The question is here explored in some detail
- **Do only sinful people suffer?**
- **Does all suffering mean we are being punished by God?**
- **Why would a righteous person suffer?**
- **How should a righteous person react to suffering?**

IS SUFFERING BETTER THAN DEATH?
Job 3:20-22 KJV
Wherefore is light given to him that is in misery, and life unto the bitter in soul;
Which long for death, but it cometh not; and dig for it more than for hid treasures;
Which rejoice exceedingly, and are glad, when they can find the grave?

Job says there are people who

---

[36] Yale Open Course Lectures, The American Revolution, Joanne Freeman, Lecture 21

"long for death" and *"are glad when they can find it."*

Even Job's wife urged him to "curse God and die"[37] in essence, committing suicide.

So here is the question:
As bad as life can sometimes be, is death better?

And a question related
Are there consequences after life, for choices made in life?

You and I would put it like this
Is there a heaven and a hell?

When Job's wife challenges him to *"curse God and die"* Job's response is that he can't do that.

1. God gave him his life. It is not his to take away
2. He knew that he would experience death in God's own time
3. Death does not end things – there is life after death

It is interesting that Job never wishes to die. He does wish that he had never been born. There is a huge difference.
- **If he had never been born, there would be no eternity and no eternal consequences however**
- **Since he has been born, it is his place to trust God through whatever suffering he had to endure.**

So far, I haven't mentioned God very much. God is assumed in the book of Job. The book begins with Job as the subject of discussion between God and Satan. Then the book enters into a section where Job and his friends talk about God and their relationship to him. The book concludes with Job and

---

[37] Job 2:9

God talking one to another. Right here is the difference in spiritual realities

- **First – the fact that God is and is involved in our lives**
- **Some people spend all their lives talking about theories of God**
- **Job finally got passed all of that to talking to God**

Religions talk about God
Christians ought to talk to God

THERE IS HOPE OF A BETTER END
Job 42:10-17 KJV

And the LORD turned the captivity of Job, when he prayed for his friends: also the LORD gave Job twice as much as he had before.
Then came there unto him all his brethren, and all his sisters, and all they that had been of his acquaintance before, and did eat bread with him in his house: and they bemoaned him, and comforted him over all the evil that the LORD had brought upon him: every man also gave him a piece of money, and every one an earring of gold.
So the LORD blessed the latter end of Job more than his beginning: for he had fourteen thousand sheep, and six thousand camels, and a thousand yoke of oxen, and a thousand she asses.
He had also seven sons and three daughters.
And he called the name of the first, Jemima; and the name of the second, Kezia; and the name of the third, Kerenhappuch.
And in all the land were no women found so fair as the daughters of Job: and their father gave them inheritance among their brethren.
After this lived Job an hundred and forty years, and saw his sons, and his sons' sons, even four generations.
So Job died, being old and full of days.

Let me make this statement as clearly as I know how to do, The Bible is not a negative book. The point of the Bible is all about hope. Every page of the Bible is designed to bring those who are in it into the world of hopefulness. And while the Bible addresses very seriously questions like,

- **Suffering**
- **Sin**
- **Satan and**
- **Death**

It is only because by confronting these things head on we can get passed them to the point of the Bible which is

- **Victory**
- **Salvation**
- **Joy and**
- **Hope**

The book of Job is a perfect first book of the Bible.

- **It gets us fully involved in the heart of human life**
- **It asks deep and probing questions that get us really grappling with meaningful things and then**
- **It leaves us with hopefulness – a reason to keep on living and keep on talking to God**

Whatever life holds today – tomorrow has HOPE.

Let me ask you – is your life characterized by hopefulness and a sense of loss?

The Bible says in Ephesians 2:12 KJV
That at that time ye were without Christ, being aliens from the commonwealth of Israel, and strangers from the covenants of promise, having no hope, and without God in the world:

If there is a sense of hopelessness it is an indication that you are

- **Without Christ and**
- **Without God**

Either you are not a saved and a stranger from God or you are saved but you are not walking with God. The good news is that you don't have to live without God in your life. He is inviting you to come to Him today and he has promised
John 6:37 KJV
All that the Father giveth me shall come to me; and him that cometh to me I will in no wise cast out.

Come to Him today. Come to Him and be saved. Come to Him and find mercy and obtain grace to help in your time of need.

Come to Him for HOPE.

Chapter Thirteen
Fundamental Concern - HELL
Isaiah 5:14

One of the fundamental questions that arises from the book of Job is whether there are consequences for choices made in this life. Some people deny that those consequences exist. They think of themselves as little more than animals.

I read with interest the last few blog entries of a man, dying of cancer. This man was an unbeliever and obnoxious against the Christian faith. His last blog said that he knew this would be his last entry before dying. In his dying strength he wanted to assure his readers that when his body went to the grave that would be it.
- **There was no spirit to meet God**
- **There was no soul to enter into heaven**
- **There was no anticipation of eternal consciousness**

He would just be – gone.

That is as much as to say,
1 Corinthians 15:32 KJV
… what advantageth it me, if the dead rise not? let us eat and drink; for to morrow we die.

The Bible categorically and authoritatively denies such sentiments and assures us that there is an eternal future. It was the fundamental question of Job. And the question is answered with both, a **fundamental concern** and a **fundamental confidence**.

I want to focus on that fundamental concern in this chapter and the fundamental confidence in the next. My outline is going to be an acrostic. I have taken the four letters that spell out the word hell, and I have assigned to each letter a word that in some way is descriptive of hell.

HELL IS HORRIBLE

There is a general lack of fear of the place called hell these days.

Illustration:

Years ago I witnessed to a relative of mine and her husband. As I spoke to them about the Lord and about how to get saved, it was very plain that my relative was under conviction and wanted to be saved, but her husband did not want anything to do with it. Neither one would get saved right then so I backed off and we began talking about other things. Later, just before we got ready to leave, my relative took me aside and said, "Marvin, I really would like to be saved, but I love my husband so much, that if he dies and goes to hell, then I want to be there with him.

The problem with that thinking is that there is not a strong enough fear of hell.

The place is horrible.

I want to show you just two verses here and one word in those two verses that I believe will describe hell's horrors for us.

A. Luke 16:23

And in hell he lift up his eyes, being in torments, and seeth Abraham afar off, and Lazarus in his bosom. (KJV)

Notice the word, "**torments**"

Webster's Dictionary defines the word as;
"to cause persistent and reoccurring distress of body and mind, to distort and twist, the infliction of torture (as on a rack), or extreme pain and anguish."

My Thesaurus gives these words as synonyms;

- **Afflict,**
- **Agonize,**
- **Crucify,**
- **Wring, and**
- **MOLEST**

My Greek dictionary traces the word back to the one where we get basement[38] from.

Doesn't that sound descriptive of hell?

All of these words render the picture of going into a torture dungeon back in England 300 years ago.

Several years ago, while we were visiting in Bremerton, the pastor there, Bro Bill Wambsgannss encouraged us to go to Vancouver BC and see the wax museum. He especially encouraged me to go into the "**Cave of Horrors**", which he said was like seeing <u>Foxes' Book of Martyrs</u> happen.

I guess I just wasn't thinking. I have tried to read <u>Foxe's Book of Martyrs</u> and got sick just reading the book. When we got to the cave, there is a warning sign outside that says it is not for the squeamish and that there was a way around without going in. *But Pastor Wambsgannss said that was the part I ought to see.* So, I went in while Anita stayed with the kids outside.

The cave is a dark and creepy tunnel fashioned in a "U" with several displays along the walls. The first display is not until you pass the first bend in the "U" and it is a pendulum with an axe blade cutting a woman in two, length ways. I had had

---

[38] I have heard that most of the children who died during the Tornado in Moore last week were in the basement of their school building. They went there for shelter from the storm only to be drowned when the pipes of the building broke.

enough. I turned around and headed back out.

But Anita about had a fit. She told me to watch the boys and she would go through. In she went and a few minutes later came out the other side.

- **Pastor Wambsgannss had told me that it was worth going to Vancouver BC just to see that one section of the wax museum.**
- **Anita had gotten enough courage to go through, and I was sure I would regret it as long as I lived if I did not go through myself.**

So, I again bolstered all of the courage I had. I entered the cave of horrors once more; this time determined that I would not exit if I did not exit out the other side. I had already seen the women in the pendulum, so I was prepared for that. I made it to a couple of others, Madam Curry who had a basket of heads freshly chopped off of bodies and was making wax likenesses of them, and a couple of others. But then I came to one with a man, hanging off a meat hook like thing going through his back and out his chest, and I had had all I could. I was not quite half way through the tunnel, but I could not bear to look at another thing. I closed my eyes and carefully felt my way out the other end, peeking only often enough to make sure I was still in the middle of the hallway and wasn't going to run into something I didn't want to run into. It was the most gruesome and horrible thing I have ever seen.

And even when it was really happening to people, it didn't hold a candle to the horrors of hell.

Now I know that I may just have a weak stomach for those kinds of things. I care so much for human life that I cannot bear the thought of anybody suffering in any way. But I also know there will be no one who is tough enough to enter into hell and not be tormented by it.

Let's look at another verse;

B. 2 Samuel 22:6

The sorrows of hell compassed me about; the snares of death prevented me; (KJV)

The word "**sorrows**" is the one I want to concentrate on for a minute.

The Hebrew word found here can be used a number of ways.
- **In its most basic of forms it means simply, "a cord or a rope" but**
- **Its most prominent use was to refer to a noose.**

The Israelites had a practice they used to humble a captured enemy; they would put
- **a sack over the enemy's head, to symbolize repentance, and**
- **a noose around their neck to symbolize submission,**

and march them through the streets.

This word **sorrows**, in their day was one used to describe being captured by the enemy or being snared by a hunter. And that is exactly what hell is. It is the snare of the Devil.

The Bible says that our adversary, the devil, *as a roaring lion, walketh about seeking whom he may devour!* (1 Peter 5:8)

Every soul that goes to hell is there as the prize of the enemy, Satan.

It is his earnest work to capture as many souls as possible and through whatever means available to him, whether lying, or trickery, or bribery, to keep people from trusting Christ as their Saviour, and thus, to condemn them to HELL.

HELL IS ETERNAL

Revelation 14:11 speaks of those who are in hell and the Lake of Fire and says;

"And the smoke of their torment ascendeth up for ever and ever: and they have no rest day nor night, who worship the beast and his image,

and whosoever receiveth the mark of his image."

We in Christian circles like to talk and sing about spending eternity with the Lord. We sing the old hymn,
> **"When we've been there ten thousand years,**
> **bright shining as the sun,**
> **we've no less days to sing God's praise**
> **than when we first begun"**

We even like to change the words sometimes and sing, "When we've been there, forever more..." And I like to sing the Chorus;
> **"I'm gonna live forever!**
> **I'm gonna die no never!**
> **Jesus died on the tree for me**
> **And I'm gonna live forever!"**

I thank the Lord for the assurance of my salvation and the assurance that with it He has given me eternal life with Him. But there is a flip side. While
- **All who have been saved will experience eternal happiness in heaven with Christ;**
- **All who are not saved will experience eternal torments in hell without Christ!**

HELL IS LITERAL
Unfortunately, many people do not think of hell as being a literal, real place

- **They talk about going through "Hell on earth" or**
- **They think that hell is not a real place but a figurative expression of how bad it is just to not be with Christ.**

I will refute that thinking with the words of the Lord Jesus Christ Himself;
A. Matthew 5:29-30
And if thy right eye offend thee, pluck it out, and cast it from thee: for it is profitable for thee that one of thy members should perish, and not

that thy whole body should be cast into hell.
And if thy right hand offend thee, cut it off, and cast it from thee: for it is profitable for thee that one of thy members should perish, and not that thy whole body should be cast into hell. (KJV)

In these verses, Jesus said that hell is so bad, and so real, that it would be better to enter into eternal life halt and maimed, than to go to hell whole. This is an exaggeration used by Jesus to teach a point. It would not help to pluck out an eye, because doing so would not help you go to heaven. And even if you were missing a part of your body on earth, when you get to heaven you would have a perfect and incorruptible body. Teachers often stretch a point to emphasize a lesson. It is a perfectly legitimate and common form of teaching and communication.

The point is, hell is real enough that a person ought to do whatever is required to escape it. Praise God, the method of escape is so much simpler than that.

Secondly Jesus said is
B. Matthew 10:28
And fear not them which kill the body, but are not able to kill the soul: but rather fear him which is able to destroy both soul and body in hell. (KJV)

Luke 12:5 says the same thing just slightly differently;
But I will forewarn you whom ye shall fear: Fear him, which after he hath killed hath power to cast into hell; yea, I say unto you, Fear him.
(KJV)

What is He saying in these two passages? He is saying that hell is as real as the person who stands before you and threatens you.

Proverbs 27:1 says,
The fear of man bringeth a snare, but whoso putteth his trust in the Lord shall be safe.

Why is it, we are so easily provoked to fear man, but seldom fear God, or fear hell? The answer is because we see the man who is standing before us as a real and immediate danger. I am saying to you this morning that hell is a very real and immediate danger for those who are without Christ.

HELL IS LOADED
Matthew 7:13 says
"Enter ye in at the strait gate,: for wide is the gate, and broad is the way that leadeth to destruction, and many there be which go in thereat"

The Bible indicates clearly that far more people go to hell than heaven.

There are a number of reasons for that. Some because God's people won't do enough to keep souls from hell. Others because they are just too proud to humble themselves and come to God. But the plain truth is, hell is loaded with people.

I asked myself as I considered this fact, who is it that will be in hell?

A. All those alive in Noah's day, except for eight people.
2 Peter 2:4-5
For if God spared not the angels that sinned, but cast them down to hell, and delivered them into chains of darkness, to be reserved unto judgment;
And spared not the old world, but saved Noah the eighth person, a preacher of righteousness, bringing in the flood upon the world of the ungodly; (KJV)

Some historians have estimated that there were as many as six billion people in the world at the time of the flood. And yet all but eight were destroyed for their wickedness.

The Bible says that as the world was in the days of Noah, so shall it be in the days when the Lord comes again to pour out God's wrath upon this earth. They were eating and drinking, and playing, and the imaginations of their hearts were only evil continually.

We are living in a day very close to that right now.

Not only are all those that died in the flood in hell,
B. So are the angels that sinned!
2 Peter 2:4
For if God spared not the angels that sinned, but cast them down to hell, and delivered them into chains of darkness, to be reserved unto judgment; (KJV)

We have already read that the Antichrist will be there too!

C. Just as God is no respecter of who He will save, hell is no respecter of who it will accept

There will be people there who were poor in this world's goods. There will also be people there who are rich in this world's goods.

Luke 16:22-23 says that the rich man died, and *in hell he lift up his eyes being in torments.*

Ezekiel 32:21 says;
The strong among the mighty shall speak to him out of the midst of hell with them that help him: they are gone down, they lie uncircumcised, slain by the sword. (KJV)

Even the strong and mighty of this world will have their delegates in hell.

In fact, one verse says that hell is continually getting bigger to hold all those that are entering into it.

Isaiah 5:14
Therefore hell hath enlarged herself, and opened her mouth without measure: and their glory, and their multitude, and their pomp, and he that rejoiceth, shall descend into it. (KJV)

And another verse says that hell reaches out to gain new inhabitants.
Isaiah 14:9
Hell from beneath is moved for thee to meet thee at thy coming: it stirreth up the dead for thee, even all the chief ones of the earth; it hath raised up from their thrones all the kings of the nations. (KJV)

- **Hell is horrible**
- **Hell is eternal**
- **Hell is literal and**
- **Hell is loaded!**

But thank the Lord there is a way of escape.

Once a person is in hell, there is no way out. The Bible says there is a great gulf fixed so that those who are there can never leave. But while we still walk this planet, while our lives are still within us, God has provided a means of escape from this horrible place called hell.

Jesus said in,
Revelation 1:18
I am he that liveth, and was dead; and, behold, I am alive for evermore, Amen; and have the keys of hell and of death. (KJV)

Jesus is the one who holds the way of escape from hell. And He is always available to deliver another person from going there.

Some people think that their lives have been so wicked, that they could never escape hell, and that God could never forgive them.

I found a verse that I believe is the answer to that for you;
Isaiah 28:18
And your covenant with death shall be disannulled, and your agreement with hell shall not stand;

The big question then, is, How do I get saved from hell? What must I do that Jesus will forgive my sins and rescue me from hell and give me a home in heaven?

The answer is wonderfully simple.
Romans 10:13 says
"For whosoever shall call upon the name of the Lord shall be saved."

You know you need to be saved, you believe that Jesus can save you, and you simply call upon Him in sincere payer and ask Him to forgive your sins and save you from hell.

The question is, will you be willing to ask Jesus to do that?

Chapter Fourteen

Fundamental Confidence – the Resurrection
Psalms 17:15 KJV

Job 19:25-26 KJV
For I know that my redeemer liveth, and that he shall stand at the latter day upon the earth:
And though after my skin worms destroy this body, yet in my flesh shall I see God:

Romans 8:18 KJV
For I reckon that the sufferings of this present time are not worthy to be compared with the glory which shall be revealed in us.

This chapter is a part of those messages that come before it. It springs from what I see as the **Fundamental Question** asked in the book of Job – *Are there consequences for deeds done in this life?*

Or – put in what I think are more useful words – *Is there a heaven and a hell?*

If eternity is not real
- **If there is no heaven**
- **If there is no hell**

Even if God exists exactly like the Bible describes Him, He is almost moot.
- **He can be all powerful**
- **He can be sovereign**
- **He can be the only Saviour**

But if when life on earth ends, life ends, He becomes for all practical purposes, irrelevant.

The question really is the fundamental, fundamental.
- **Is eternity real?**
- **Are there consequences for actions in this life?**

If not we may as well do as some have suggested and "Eat drink and be merry, for tomorrow, we die."

I began to answer that "fundamental question" last chapter, with a message on the subject of hell. I want to address the other side of the subject with a chapter I am calling: "**The Fundamental Confidence.**"

That confidence is dividable into three parts; represented by the passages I began the message with this morning.

THERE IS A RESURRECTION FROM THE DEAD
Psalms 17:15 KJV
As for me, I will behold thy face in righteousness: I shall be satisfied, when I awake, with thy likeness.

We think of King David as an incredibly blessed man.
- **He was the greatest King in Israel's history**
- **He was a valiant warrior who even defeated a giant with just a slingshot**
- **He built a great palace to live in**
- **He is remembered with fondness among the Jews even to this day**

But that view of David is seen through rose colored glasses.

The fact is David's life was one of horrible stress and difficulty. Read through the Psalms, mostly written by David – and you will see a man who constantly admits to being surrounded by enemies weighing in on him daily.

- **He frequently goes to sleep with tears watering his pillow**
- **He has heartbreak after heartbreak throughout his life**

One of his last living acts was to settle a dispute between a son who wanted to be king and the son David had determined to be king.

And in his last few breaths King David warned King Solomon of all of the men – still living – who had pretended to be his friends but were in truth, enemies.

And the thing is, David did have options:
He could have contented himself to be a musician for Saul, kept his nose clean, and simply existed as a court servant.

Later on, he fled to Gath and was befriended by Achish, the King of Gath. Once there, Saul stopped chasing him and things got pretty good.
He could have lived out the rest of his life as a citizen of Gath, leading his own band of men, separated from the rest of the Philistines but safe from King Saul.

The only trouble was – **David was a believer.**
And the struggles he experienced were directly related to his being a believer. Saul wanted to kill him because God had anointed David to be the next King after Saul. And Gath – in order for David to stay there, he would have had to vex his soul with worldly compromises. No believer can live a worldly lifestyle without it killing his soul.

So why would David choose to live for God even though living for God meant so much pain and suffering? Because he was convinced that,
Psalms 17:15 KJV
As for me, I will behold thy face in righteousness: I shall be satisfied, when I awake, with thy likeness.

He knew there would be a resurrection of the righteous.

ETERNAL HEAVEN AWAITS THE BELIEVER
Job 19:25-26 KJV

For I know that my redeemer liveth, and that he shall stand at the latter day upon the earth:
And though after my skin worms destroy this body, yet in my flesh shall I see God:

King David was convinced that he would awake in God's likeness.

Job was convinced that, though he would die – he would be resurrected to see God. So more than life after death – it is life after death, with God.
- **It is not nirvana**
- **It is not a collective consciousness**
- **It is not limbo**

It is real life. It is physical life .

Job said, *"in my flesh, shall I see God."* In the resurrection, this body, which goes to the graver, becomes the seed that produces the bodies we have in heaven.
- **It is not this body – exactly**
- **But it is this body – essentially**

1 Corinthians 15:35-37 KJV
But some man will say, How are the dead raised up? and with what body do they come?
Thou fool, that which thou sowest is not quickened, except it die:
And that which thou sowest, thou sowest not that body that shall be, but bare grain, it may chance of wheat, or of some other grain:

I can't give you the specifics of how it works any more than a farmer can give you the specifics of how he can plant one kernel of corn and from it grows a plant that produces hundreds of new kernels of corn.

But it does happen.

The Bible goes on to explain that, just like there are different types of flesh on earth:
- **The meat of a cow is different than**

- **The meat of a bird which is different than**
- **The meat of a fish**

So, the Bible says
1 Corinthians 15:39-40 KJV
All flesh is not the same flesh: but there is one kind of flesh of men, another flesh of beasts, another of fishes, and another of birds.
There are also celestial bodies, and bodies terrestrial: but the glory of the celestial is one, and the glory of the terrestrial is another.

- **There is one body that is at home on this earth - terrestrial**
- **There is another body that is at home in heaven - celestial**

Further the Bible says,
1 Corinthians 15:41-42 KJV
There is one glory of the sun, and another glory of the moon, and another glory of the stars: for one star differeth from another star in glory.
So also is the resurrection of the dead. It is sown in corruption; it is raised in incorruption:

- **The body that is at home on this earth is corrupt**
- **The body that is at home in heaven is incorrupt**

Since the earthly body is corrupt (sinful) and sin, when it is finished "*bringeth forth death*" this earthly body dies. But the one that raises from the grave is incorrupt and will never die
1 Corinthians 15:53-54 KJV
For this corruptible must put on incorruption, and this mortal must put on immortality.
So when this corruptible shall have put on incorruption, and this mortal shall have put on immortality, then shall be brought to pass the saying that is written, Death is swallowed up in victory.

David knew there was a resurrection
Job knew that resurrection to be real and physical – into the presence of God in heaven.

HEAVEN IS MORE GLORIOUS THAN EARTH CAN IMAGINE

Romans 8:18 KJV

For I reckon that the sufferings of this present time are not worthy to be compared with the glory which shall be revealed in us.

The book of Job is probably the oldest written document in existence today. The very first thing we learn about human history is that Job suffered for no apparent reason.

Debates go back and forth through the book concerning whether Job had somehow provoked God to such suffering and his wife even suggested that he should just curse God and die. But Job had to stay faithful to God

- **He was sure that there were consequences for actions**
- **He was sure there was life after death**
- **He was sure he would raise from the grave to meet God**

And I think he already knew what Apostle Paul said so many years later…

That regardless of however bad this world might be, *"the sufferings of this present world are not worthy to be compared with the glory which shall be revealed in us."*

- **A place without pain, sin, sickness, death or suffering**
- **A place where Christians are eternally rewarded for their faithfulness while on earth and**
- **A place where the greatest joy will be unhindered fellowship with God the Father and His Son, Jesus Christ**

This then is the fundamental, fundamental.

This is the one absolute truth that is life changing.

- **This is the doctrine that transformed a shepherd boy into the most famous king of all time**
- **This is the doctrine that sustained Job despite the most difficult trials imaginable – and brought him through to great blessings after.**

- **This is the doctrine that changed a religious zealot like the Saul of Tarsus into the most influential Christian since Jesus Christ, Apostle Paul**

This is fundamentally fundamental; it is the basis for all Christian faith and conversation. This one truth,
- **That there is a resurrection from the dead,**
- **That eternal heaven awaits the believer and**
- **That it is more glorious than this earth can imagine,**
motivates men and women of faith.

Or else means nothing to those who are false professors. They will claim to be Christians, but their lives can't prove it.

Fundamentals Concerning Christ

Chapter Fifteen

The Fullness of Time
Galatians 4:1-7 KJV

The Bible tells us 1 Timothy 4:1 KJV
Now the Spirit speaketh expressly, that in the latter times some shall depart from the faith, giving heed to seducing spirits, and doctrines of devils;

Further 2 Timothy 4:3-4 KJV says
For the time will come when they will not endure sound doctrine; but after their own lusts shall they heap to themselves teachers, having itching ears;
And they shall turn away their ears from the truth, and shall be turned unto fables.

This departure from the faith will be so widespread at the end that Jesus said,
Luke 18:8 KJV
….. when the Son of man cometh, shall he find faith on the earth?

When Jesus returns, we know there will be a type of faith. People will give heed to,
- **Seducing spirits**
- **Doctrines of Devils and**
- **Silly fables**

So, when Jesus comes again there will be a faith, but it won't be a correct faith.

The word faith has a depth of meaning to it:
- **Faith … A persuasion**
- **Faith… A spiritual kin to hope**
- **Faith… A defined belief or set of doctrines**

I am convinced that it is the third of these Jesus addressed in His question; *"**When the Son of man comes, will he find people who believe the doctrines that were once delivered to them?**"*

The obvious implication of the question is "No."
When Jesus returns,
- **So many people will have departed from the faith**
- **So many people will have rejected sound doctrine**
- **So many people will have heaped to themselves their own brand of teachers**

That there will be none to very few left on this earth who believe the doctrines Jesus originally delivered to the Apostles.

I do not believe it is possible to reverse the prophecies of these passages. But neither do I believe I have to contribute to them.
- **I can resist the spirit of the world that seduces me away from God**
- **I can avoid the doctrines of devils by hearing sound doctrine preached**
- **I can turn from silly fables instead of turning away from the faith of Christ**

I can be salt and light. I do not have to blend in to the world like a chameleon.

That has been the motivation and purpose for this book... to clarify and strengthen faith. I began with what seems to me to be the beginning: **God**. We know that God is, but we need to know who God is and what He is like.

I moved from there to: the **Bible**. The only authoritative source for an understanding of God is His own message to man. Anything other than the Bible is only guesswork and we don't need that. We need the truth – straight from God's mouth.

From there I spent some time on what I believe is the "fundamental question;" *Are there consequences for actions done in this life?* or in other words, *Is there a heaven to gain and a hell to shun?*

The Bible clearly teaches,
- **That there is life after death**
- **That heaven exists for the righteous but**
- **That hell is the destination of the lost and further**
- **That there is an abundant entrance into heaven versus being saved yet so as by fire.**

I have been trying to lay this argument out in the same order I think I find it in the Bible. The Old Testament sets up this dilemma:
- **There is a living and Holy God**
- **Man's actions have turned God's face from us**
- **We are in this desperate need of salvation**

And the answer for that need is given to us in the New Testament; the answer is Jesus Christ.

That brings me then to the next set of subjects I would like to address – What the Bible says about Jesus Christ. And I want to begin with Galatians 4:4 KJV

But when the fulness of the time was come, God sent forth his Son, made of a woman, made under the law,

THE WISDOM OF GOD - fullness
But when the fullness of time was come…

God the Father sent His Son to be the Saviour of the world at just the right moment in time
- **It was not too soon or else man would not be convinced of His sin**
- **It was not too late or else there would be no one who could be saved**

One of the worst things about our corrupt natures is that we always think we are smarter than God.

- **If some of us were God, we would be much tougher than He is**
- **If others of us were God, we would be much more lenient than He is**

If some of us were God, we would have wanted to save mankind before Satan tempted Eve

Some of don't think God is very wise at all

- **We don't like the way He has allowed the devil to tempt men**
- **We don't like the way He has given the kingdoms of this world away**
- **We don't like that He has allowed so many different types of religions**
- **We don't like that He allowed religious people to kill religious people over the centuries since Jesus died**

Isn't it the truth that you wrestle with,

- **Why church?**
- **Why the Bible?**
- **Why baptism?**
- **Why standards of dress and conduct?**

We wonder:

- **Why did Jesus come in the middle of the Roman occupation of Israel?**
- **Why couldn't Jesus have spared them from the Roman destruction of Jerusalem?**
- **Why did Jesus come at just the time when the Jews would almost certainly reject Him?**

We go on questioning:

- **Why doesn't God just tell me what to believe?**
- **Why doesn't God just judge all of the sinners and reward all of the Christians?**

Don't you ask these sorts of questions?

It's the corrupt sin nature that breeds those question into our minds

1 Corinthians 1:18-25 KJV

For the preaching of the cross is to them that perish foolishness; but unto us which are saved it is the power of God.

For it is written, I will destroy the wisdom of the wise, and will bring to nothing the understanding of the prudent.

Where is the wise? where is the scribe? where is the disputer of this world? hath not God made foolish the wisdom of this world?

For after that in the wisdom of God the world by wisdom knew not God, it pleased God by the foolishness of preaching to save them that believe.

For the Jews require a sign, and the Greeks seek after wisdom:

But we preach Christ crucified, unto the Jews a stumblingblock, and unto the Greeks foolishness;

But unto them which are called, both Jews and Greeks, Christ the power of God, and the wisdom of God.

Because the foolishness of God is wiser than men; and the weakness of God is stronger than men.

Faith trusts the wisdom of God.

And it was in His wisdom that God selected just the right time to send His Son into the world.

You have a clear choice.
- **Will you trust the wisdom of God and believe on Jesus Christ as your Saviour?**
- **Will you trust the wisdom of God and obey what He has taught us in the Bible or**
- **Will you trust the wisdom of this world – your own wisdom and stumble at the Word of God?**

The wisdom of God in knowing the fullness of time.

THE GRACE OF GOD - his Son

Galatians 4:4 KJV

But when the fulness of the time was come, God sent forth his Son, made of a woman, made under the law,

There are three descriptors of this gift of God in Sending
Jesus
- **The who**
- **The how and**
- **The when**

A. The Who
"God sent forth His Son"

Not a servant, not a slave and not even an angel.

- **When God gave so that you and I could be forgiven our sins
  and reconciled to God.**
- **When God gave so that we could be free from the
  consequences of our sin and**
- **When God gave so that we could go to heaven and not to hell**

God gave His Son.

Giving Christ was the only thing God could give that would
have cost Him
- **He owns the cattle on a thousand hills**
- **All the silver and gold is His**
- **He supplies our needs our of His "riches in glory."**

God could have given wealth and riches and material things
forever and never have cost Him a thing. But when God sent
His Son, He paid the price of our salvation.

B. The How
"made of a woman"

Two thoughts here:
- **That God became a human**
- **That a human was involved in God becoming human**

It is the grace of God that gives us a responsibility in the plan
of God.

For Mary, her place created,
- <u>**Tensions**</u> **as her life plans got changed**

- **Misunderstandings** as Joseph was minded to put her away for the pregnancy and
- **Heartache** as she watched her Son die for the sins of the world

That isn't a lot different than when you serve God, is it?
- **When you surrender to live for God your own plans change**
- **When you surrender to live for God some of your friends and family misunderstand**
- **When you surrender to live for God you'll go through the heartache of seeing some you love turn from the faith**

But despite all of the troubles Mary experienced being the mother of Jesus; she was still the mother of Jesus. It is a gracious thing that God allows us to be responsible in serving the Lord.

C. The When
made under the law

The significance of that is that God didn't skirt the issues to save us but confronted them head on. The law was there to show us we could not save ourselves.

But when Jesus was made under the law God showed us One Who was so much better than the law that
- **He fulfilled the law and then**
- **Nailed the law to His cross, removing it forever from coming between us and God**

God has no intention of sweeping your own sins under the carpet. His purpose is to confront your sin and deal with it. He wants to nail your sin to His cross that it is removed from your life forever.

THE COMPASSION OF GOD – to redeem
Galatians 4:4-5 KJV
But when the fulness of the time was come, God sent forth his Son, made of a woman, made under the law,

To redeem them that were under the law, that we might receive the adoption of sons.

Let me attempt to rephrase this whole chapter one last time before we finish

Our problem – the consequences of our sin has separated between us and God.

Our condition – God's Word has announced to us that we are condemned to an eternal hell because of our sin.

Our salvation – But at just the right time, God sent His Son into this world, so that you and I might be saved, Galatians 4:5 calls it redeemed; rescued from the penalty of sin.

God did not have to send us a Saviour any more than you have to be saved. But He did send Jesus as our Saviour and you can be saved today – right now – if you will.

Chapter Sixteen

There are three; they are one
1 John 5:1-7 KJV

The book of 1 John is perhaps one of the best liked and easy to read pieces of all of the New Testament. It was written by the Apostle John somewhere near 90 AD. By this time John was an old man, nearly 90 years old himself.

Though he and his brother James were once nicknamed Boanerges "Sons of Thunder" because they asked permission of the Lord to call down fire from heaven and consume some people they perceived as enemies, John was later known as "The Apostle whom Jesus loved" and traditions says that in his last days the younger men of the church would lead him to the pulpit where he would sit down and say the very same thing every time, that they should, "love one another" a phrase he repeats five times in 1 John.

Someone is supposed to have asked him why he kept repeating the same thing over and over. His reply was, "It is the Lord's command. And if this alone be done it is enough."[39] It makes us think of John as being soft sort of guy in his old age.

A casual reading of 1 John tends to interpret it softly. In fact 1, 2 and 3 John are all written to counter heresies that were becoming an increasing problem in the churches near the turn of the century.

While 1 John is written with a gracious hand, it is not written with a soft, wishy-washy hand. Look again at some select verses in this short letter:

---

[39] http://www.biblepath.com/john1.html, accessed 6-22-13

1 John 1:6 KJV
If we say that we have fellowship with him, and walk in darkness, we lie, and do not the truth:

1 John 2:9 KJV
He that saith he is in the light, and hateth his brother, is in darkness even until now.

1 John 3:8 KJV
He that committeth sin is of the devil; for the devil sinneth from the beginning. For this purpose the Son of God was manifested, that he might destroy the works of the devil.

1 John 4:1 KJV
Beloved, believe not every spirit, but try the spirits whether they are of God: because many false prophets are gone out into the world.

And jumping to
2 John 1:9-10 KJV
Whosoever transgresseth, and abideth not in the doctrine of Christ, hath not God. He that abideth in the doctrine of Christ, he hath both the Father and the Son.
If there come any unto you, and bring not this doctrine, receive him not into your house, neither bid him God speed:

These are some very pointed and direct statements, are they not? Those who were in my Sunday School class today learned about some of those early heresies and false prophets.

John's letters target in particular heresies having to do with the deity of Christ. The heresies took on a number of different styles but some of the ideas that were being preached were,

- **That Jesus was never a human but only appeared to be human.**
- **That Jesus' humanity and deity merged but that the Spirit of God came upon baby Jesus shortly after He was born and left him just before He was crucified and**
- **That Jesus was a god but a lesser God than God the Father**

It was into this fray that the old Apostle wrote the words of,
1 John 5:7
For there are three that bear record in heaven, the Father, the Word and the Holy Ghost; and these three are one.

A CONTROVERSIAL DOCTRINE
1 John 5:7
For there are three that bear record in heaven, the Father, the Word and the Holy Ghost; and these three are one.

Just as there were heresies concerning the deity of Christ in the first century, there are similar heresies today.

A. The Pentecostals
The official doctrine of the United Pentecostals is something called modalism. The idea is that God take on the form of
- **God the Father sometimes**
- **God the Son sometimes and**
- **God the Holy Spirit sometimes**

One of the most popular preachers on the Television these days is T.D. Jakes. He speaks to crowds of thousands all over the country. Jakes was recently put on the hot seat because his church's official position is modalism. Jakes denied being an extreme modalist. But could not deny taking a moderate modalistic position.

One of the reasons I advise against watching the TV evangelists or listening to them on the radio is that, just because they sound good and are popular – you could be getting fed, very subtle but very bad doctrine.

B. The Jehovah's Witnesses
The Jehovah's Witnesses have gone so far as to write their own version of the Bible in order to reinforce their own doctrine that Jesus Christ is a lesser god than God the Father.

Our Bible says in
John 1:1 KJV
In the beginning was the Word, and the Word was with God, and the Word was God.

They have re-written that to read
John 1:1 NWT
In the beginning the Word was, and the Word was with God, and the Word was a god. They inserted the indefinite article "a" and they changed the capitol G in the last word to a small god.

"In the beginning the Word was, and the Word was with [capital G, BIG] God, and the Word was a [lower case g, LESSER] god."

C. The Mormons
Teach that Jesus is a created being and brother to Lucifer.

They teach that God is an evolving being.
- **God the Father has evolved into the highest order of being**
- **God the son has evolved into a higher order than man but not quite as high as God the Father and**
- **Any man can evolve into god through time and obedience to the faith[40]**

And of course there are varying degrees of these and other heresies taught in one place or another.

If the doctrine of the deity of Christ is controversial, then we could certainly call this verse
A CONTROVERSIAL PASSAGE
1 John 5:7
For there are three that bear record in heaven, the Father, the Word and the Holy Ghost; and these three are one.

---

[40] "What man is God once was, what God is, man may become."

Albert Barnes writes

"There is no passage of the New Testament which has given rise to so much discussion in regard to its genuineness as this. The … importance of the verse in its bearing on the doctrine of the Trinity has contributed to this, …

On the one hand, the clear testimony which it seems to bear to the doctrine of the Trinity, has made that portion of the Christian church which holds the doctrine reluctant in the highest degree to abandon it; and

On the other hand, the same clearness of the testimony to that doctrine, has made those who deny it not less reluctant to admit the genuineness of the passage."

No other version of the Bible than the King James Bible includes this verse without qualification. And most other versions completely leave it out. Why? Because if it is Bible it destroys the heresies concerning the deity of Christ.

- **It is so very clear**
- **It is so very precise**
- **It is so absolutely plain**

that a person cannot misunderstand it; you either have to accept that:

There are three that bear record in heaven

- **The Father**
- **The Word and**
- **The Holy Ghost**

and furthermore that,

- **These three are one**

Or else you have to challenge the authority of the verse itself.

A CONSISTENT TRUTH

1 John 5:7

For there are three that bear record in heaven, the Father, the Word and the Holy Ghost; and these three are one.

What is taught in this verse is taught throughout the Bible, though nowhere so clearly as here.

A. There are three
1. There are three *Persons*
- **God the Father**
- **God the Son**
- **God the Holy Ghost**

Can anyone deny that these three Persons all are found in the pages of the Bible? Though seldom are they found together in the same verse, and I want to save those references for a moment.

- **They are each found in the Bible and**
- **They are each found to be God**

2. There are three *Positions*
The Father Sent the Son
John 3:16 KJV
For God so loved the world, that he gave his only begotten Son, that whosoever believeth in him should not perish, but have everlasting life.

The Son Sent the Spirit
John 15:26 KJV
But when the Comforter is come, whom I will send unto you from the Father, even the Spirit of truth, which proceedeth from the Father, he shall testify of me:

The Spirit speaks only what He hears
John 16:13 KJV
Howbeit when he, the Spirit of truth, is come, he will guide you into all truth: for he shall not speak of himself; but whatsoever he shall hear, that shall he speak: and he will shew you things to come.

3. There are three *Performances*
1 Peter 1:2 KJV

Elect according to the foreknowledge of God the Father, through sanctification of the Spirit, unto obedience and sprinkling of the blood of Jesus Christ: Grace unto you, and peace, be multiplied.

The Father planned our salvation
According to the foreknowledge of God the Father

The Son paid for our salvation
Sprinkling of the blood of Jesus Christ

The Spirit performed our salvation
through sanctification of the Spirit

4. There are three *Places*
Matthew 3:16-17 KJV
And Jesus, when he was baptized, went up straightway out of the water: and, lo, the heavens were opened unto him, and he saw the Spirit of God descending like a dove, and lighting upon him:
And lo a voice from heaven, saying, This is my beloved Son, in whom I am well pleased.

The Father spoke
This is my beloved Son, in whom I am well pleased.

The Son was baptized
And Jesus, when he was baptized

The Spirit descended
and he saw the Spirit of God descending like a dove, and lighting upon him

Here is the great argument against modalism. (That God is one God who manifests Himself in different forms as necessary.) In Matthew 3, God was all three persons at the same time and same place.

B. These three *are* one
This bold statement of 1 John 5:7 is confirmed in verses such as

Colossians 2:9 KJV
For in him dwelleth all the fulness of the Godhead bodily.

There is a Godhead; the three Persons. But in Jesus Christ dwells not just one part of that Godhead, but all the fullness of the Godhead.

There are Three and they are One.

So what's the point of all of this?

1 John 5:7-14 KJV
For there are three that bear record in heaven, the Father, the Word, and the Holy Ghost: and these three are one.
And there are three that bear witness in earth, the Spirit, and the water, and the blood: and these three agree in one.
If we receive the witness of men, the witness of God is greater: for this is the witness of God which he hath testified of his Son.
He that believeth on the Son of God hath the witness in himself: he that believeth not God hath made him a liar; because he believeth not the record that God gave of his Son.
And this is the record, that God hath given to us eternal life, and this life is in his Son.
He that hath the Son hath life; and he that hath not the Son of God hath not life.
These things have I written unto you that believe on the name of the Son of God; that ye may know that ye have eternal life, and that ye may believe on the name of the Son of God.
And this is the confidence that we have in him, that, if we ask any thing according to his will, he heareth us:

Can you see how simple this passage is?
1. God the Father, God the Son and God the Holy Spirit all bear record and testify that Jesus Christ is the Son of God
2. If you believe that Jesus Christ is the Son of God you can know you have eternal life and
3. You can be confident that, if you ask Him to, He will forgive you of your sins and save you from hell

But the warning is also there
He that hath the Son hath life; and he that hath not the Son of God hath not life.

Eternal salvation or damnation hangs in the balance. Heaven or hell rests right here. God the Father, God the Word and God the Holy Spirit have all told us that Jesus Christ is the way to have eternal life.
- **Will we believe Him?**
- **Will we come to Christ as our only hope of Salvation?**

And for those who are saved,
- *Will we bear the record of Their record to the souls of men and women around us?*

Chapter Seventeen
Behold the Lamb
John 1:14-29 KJV

I am forever impressed with how long the Roman civilization actually lasted. It really existed in about four different phases before it eventually collapsed:
- **The Roman kingdom lasted about 250 years**
- **The Roman Republic lasted about 479 years**
- **The Western Roman Empire lasted about 500 years**
- **The Eastern Roman Empire lasted another 1000 years**

I began comparing that to the history of the United States.
Even is we wanted to take our history back all the way to 1492[41] (and really we should only go back to 1607[42]) the history of the United States is less than a quarter of that of the Roman Empire and, counting every moment a person of English descent lived on this continent, our country hasn't existed as long as either of the two most well known phases in Roman history.[43]

As I see it, Rome, began a state of decline in about 45 BC, when Julius Caesar came into power and changed Roman government from a Republic to an Empire. The Empire reached their zenith of power under Caesar Augustus, just before Christ was born – But they quickly fell into a state of decay with one Caesar after the other being assassinated.

---

[41] When Columbus sailed to America; giving us a history spanning approx. 521 years.

[42] When the city of Jamestown, Virginia was settled; giving us a history of 406 years.

[43] The Roman Republic, upon which our founding fathers built the United States Constitution and the Roman Empire, in the midst of which Christianity was born and grew in Europe.

Israel had been conquered by them about 63 years before the birth of Christ. When you add to this the spiritual wickedness of the day it is not difficult to see that the Jews were an oppressed and broken people, dying for a glimmer of hope.

Now it is thirty years after Christ's birth, nearly 100 years of Roman occupation (compare that to our 237 year history). One day John the Baptist looks out over the multitudes of people who had come to be baptized of him and he cries out: John 1:29 KJV

…. Behold the Lamb of God, which taketh away the sin of the world.
This was "good news" beyond our imagination.

Notice with me three things about this short announcement:
ANTICIPATION
"Behold"

Remember that the people had longed for this for something like 4000 years. Ever since God had promised in Genesis 3:15 KJV

And I will put enmity between thee and the woman, and between thy seed and her seed; it shall bruise thy head, and thou shalt bruise his heel.
God's faithful believers had lived in anticipation and expectation of the day when One who was born of a woman but not of man – would come to conquer the effects of sin in this world.

You can imagine that after 4000 years; a lot of people had given up hope. But you can also imagine that those who still believed the promise of the Lord would have been desperate right about then.

The times were tough just then,
- **The Roman occupation**
- **The Religious corruption**
- **The sinful degeneration**

Had left the nation of Jews hungry for an answer. Faithful people like

- **Simeon and**
- **Anna the prophetess and**
- **John the Baptist**

had kept their eyes open. At the birth of Christ:

Simeon took the baby up and said, "*Lord, now lettest thou thy servant depart in peace, according to thy word:*
For mine eyes have seen thy salvation,
Which thou hast prepared before the face of all people;
A light to lighten the Gentiles, and the glory of thy people Israel."[44]
And when **Anna** saw him the Bible says she, "*... gave thanks likewise unto the Lord, and spake of him to all them that looked for redemption in Jerusalem.*"[45]

John the Baptist came of age 30 years after them, but his reaction is exactly they same as theirs; Jesus coming was to them – the answer of the prayers of their people from the beginning of time.

I think we are in a time very much like that right now. Though our history is not nearly so long as was theirs, I am grieving for our country and for our world. We have gone from a state of hopefulness to one of anxiousness over what is happening in America.

Remember, the Christians did not come to America because they saw it as a land of opportunity. They did not come here because they believed here they could

- **Get land**
- **Gain wealth and**
- **Become successful**

They came here because they saw in this land the opportunity to worship God freely and without fear of oppression and persecution.

---

[44] Luke 2:29-32 KJV
[45] Luke 2:38 KJV

We are watching as those very liberties are being methodically removed from the fabric of America. I'll tell you what that is doing to me; it is causing me to remember that

- **My hope is built on nothing less than Jesus blood and righteousness.**
- **It is calling me back to the Word of God and to Titus 2:13 KJV**
  Looking for that blessed hope, and the glorious appearing of the great God and our Saviour Jesus Christ;

John the Baptist looks up that day and calls out to the multitutdes, *"Behold! The Lamb of God which taketh away the sin of the world."*

SUBSTITUTION
"The Lamb of God"

There is in the cry of the Baptist, a foreshadowing of the difficult work Jesus had come to do. This phrase would have taken every Jewish mind all the way back to the book of Genesis when God tempted Abraham and told him to take Isaac, his son to Mount Mariah and there offer him as a sacrifice.

As Abraham and Isaac climbed the slopes of the mountain Isaac, who was plenty old enough to understand what was going on, said to his father, "We have the fire and we have the wood. Father, where is the sacrifice?" To which Abraham replied in Genesis 22:8 KJV
... My son, God will provide himself a lamb for a burnt offering: ...

Abraham was willing to obey God and offer his son. But he believed God would provide His own sacrifice.

This principle that God would one day provide His own Lamb as a Sacrifice carries through the Bible.

Isaiah 53:7-8 KJV says of Jesus Christ:
He was oppressed, and he was afflicted, yet he opened not his mouth: he is brought as a lamb to the slaughter, and as a sheep before her shearers is dumb, so he openeth not his mouth.
He was taken from prison and from judgment: and who shall declare his generation? for he was cut off out of the land of the living: for the transgression of my people was he stricken.

Notice that last phrase:
for the transgression of my people was he stricken.

Isaiah 53:5 KJV says,
But he was wounded for our transgressions, he was bruised for our iniquities: the chastisement of our peace was upon him; and with his stripes we are healed.

He came to be our substitute. Like Isaac, we were condemned, on our way to death.
Romans 3:9-12 KJV says
What then? are we better than they? No, in no wise: for we have before proved both Jews and Gentiles, that they are all under sin;
As it is written, There is none righteous, no, not one:
There is none that understandeth, there is none that seeketh after God.
They are all gone out of the way, they are together become unprofitable; there is none that doeth good, no, not one.

Romans 3:23 KJV
For all have sinned, and come short of the glory of God;

Romans 6:23 KJV
For the wages of sin is death; ….

But before death could happen God Himself provided a substitute; One who would die for us.
Romans 5:8 KJV
But God commendeth his love toward us, in that, while we were yet sinners, Christ died for us.

Do you think it is any accident that John the Baptist spoke those words: *Behold, the Lamb of God…?* Not on your life. He knew Jesus would be our substitute. He would die for our sins.

SATISFACTION
"that taketh away the sin of the world"

Notice, John the Baptist said that Jesus came to take away the sin of the world
- **Not to defeat the Romans**
- **Not to set the religious system straight**
- **Not to make them wealthy**
- **Not to restore their national pride**

Jesus came to take away their sin.

If we would remember that, we could avoid a lot of confusion and disillusionment with our faith.
- **God's purpose is not to give us good leaders**
- **God's heart is not to grant us great favor with world governments**

God's love for us has one all overriding concern – He was to take away our sins.

What is the big deal about our sin?
A. Our sin has separated us from God
Isaiah 59:2 KJV
But your iniquities have separated between you and your God, and your sins have hid his face from you, that he will not hear.

B. Our sin has set us at enmity with God
Romans 8:7 KJV
Because the carnal mind is enmity against God: for it is not subject to the law of God, neither indeed can be.

Notice that the enmity is against God. It is God who is offended. It is God we need to make things right with.

C. Our sin will by no means go unpunished

Numbers 14:18 KJV
The LORD is longsuffering, and of great mercy, forgiving iniquity and transgression, and by no means clearing the guilty, visiting the iniquity of the fathers upon the children unto the third and fourth generation.

Here is where the rubber meets the road: while God is longsuffering and merciful – sin always gets punished.
- **You are not going to get around it**
- **You are not going to escape it**
- **You are not going to get God to ignore it**

That's why it is a big deal that Jesus "*taketh away the sin of the world.*"

D. Jesus came to be our substitute
- **Taking the judgment of our sin upon himself and**
- *Satisfying* **the justice of God**

1 John 4:10 KJV
Herein is love, not that we loved God, but that he loved us, and sent his Son to be the propitiation for our sins.

The word propitiation means "the act of appeasing." When Jesus died on the cross, He satisfied all of God's righteous demands against our sin.

2 Corinthians 5:21 KJV
For he hath made him to be sin for us, who knew no sin; that we might be made the righteousness of God in him.

John 1:29 KJV
…. Behold the Lamb of God, which taketh away the sin of the world.

That's good news!

Chapter Eighteen

My Beloved Son
Matthew 3:13-17 KJV

Sometimes the simplest of things are the most important of things.

- **A small spring fastened in just the right place under the car's hood may be all that stands between running and broke down**
- **A change of just one digit on a speed limit sign can mean the difference between a ticket and an ordinary day on the road**
- **I have a clock at home that requires I pull three brass chains and once per week. Doing that simple step is the difference between telling time and looking at a piece of decoration**

Simple things can sometimes be very important things.

We have before us an incredibly simple passage describing the Baptism of Jesus Christ.

- **It is so simple that many people pass over it without a second thought**
- **It is so simple that a lot of people see no significance in the passage to themselves or their own spiritual life**
- **It is such a simple act, the baptism of Jesus Christ, that the majority of people refuse to follow the pattern that was set by our Lord at His own baptism.**

It is a simple passage that

- **Demonstrates the Scriptural practice of Christian baptism**
- **Teaches us the Biblical reason behind Christian baptism and**
- **Reveals to us the depth of Christ's relationship to God the Father**

There was John the Baptist, the cousin of Jesus Christ - he was just six months older than the Lord. That means his ministry must not have been much more than six months old because Jewish custom would have prevented either of them from entering a public arena before age thirty.

We have no explanation other than the hand of God as to why so many multitudes of people had heard of John the Baptist or why they were going out to hear him preach.

- **It wasn't his slick advertizing**
- **It wasn't his charismatic presentation**
- **It wasn't his hard work in promoting his meetings**

The only thing that can explain the huge numbers of people who were traveling from Jerusalem down to the Jordan River to hear John preach and be baptized of him is that God was calling them out.

We have no idea how many were out there with John the Baptist; the Bible says it was, "Jerusalem and all Judea and all the region round about Jordan".[46] Even if it is not everybody, that's a huge crowd!

And then came the day Jesus presented himself to John.

John the Baptist knew He would come, but he still did not feel worthy to do the work he was called to do.

There is a lesson there for us all:
I am more concerned about the person who thinks he is qualified to do the ministry than the one who knows he is not; but *we must not allow our own shortcomings prevent us from doing what God calls us to do*.

After some discussion John the Baptist and Jesus Christ went down into the water together, where Jesus was baptized.

This picture of baptism is potent.

- **They went into the Jordan River**
- **Jesus was baptized and**
- **Came up straightway out of the water**

---

[46] Matthew 3:5

Just the mental image of this baptism tells me that Jesus was fully submerged under the water in the act of baptism. Never forget that the word baptism itself means to be immersed. Scriptural Baptism is always performed,

- **By a Biblical authority (the local Baptist church)**
- **Of a Biblical candidate (a saved person)**
- **Using a Biblical method (full immersion under water)**

I see Jesus'
RELATIONSHIP THROUGH ETERNITY
Matthew 3:17 KJV
And lo a voice from heaven, saying, This is my beloved Son, in whom I am well pleased.

In a touching scene we find here the first reference in the New Testament of Jesus Christ being called the Son of God. The angel had told Mary that the child she would conceive would be of the Holy Ghost. When Jesus was just twelve years old, He made reference to His Father's business. But now we have God the Father pointing out Jesus Christ and saying
"This is my beloved Son."

The sonship of Jesus Christ goes all the way back to Genesis 3:15 when God promised that the seed of the woman would bruise the head of the Serpent.
Genesis 3:14-15 KJV
And the LORD God said unto the serpent, Because thou hast done this, thou art cursed above all cattle, and above every beast of the field; upon thy belly shalt thou go, and dust shalt thou eat all the days of thy life:
And I will put enmity between thee and the woman, and between thy seed and her seed; it shall bruise thy head, and thou shalt bruise his heel.

There is a subtle hint in this promise that though not seen in a casual reading, has been noticed and observed by Jewish and Christian students all through the centuries, the One who would defeat Satan would be the seed of a woman and not the seed of a man.

Daniel prophesied about this same truth when he interpreted Nebuchadnezzar's dream. He told the king that God had revealed to him the major kingdoms that would come in this world

- **Nebuchadnezzar was the first**
- **There would be a second and**
- **A third and**
- **A final fourth kingdom**

then Daniel said

Daniel 2:34 KJV

Thou sawest till that a stone was cut out without hands, which smote the image upon his feet that were of iron and clay, and brake them to pieces.

Daniel 2:44-45 KJV

And in the days of these kings shall the God of heaven set up a kingdom, which shall never be destroyed: and the kingdom shall not be left to other people, but it shall break in pieces and consume all these kingdoms, and it shall stand for ever.
Forasmuch as thou sawest that the stone was cut out of the mountain without hands, and that it brake in pieces the iron, the brass, the clay, the silver, and the gold; the great God hath made known to the king what shall come to pass hereafter: and the dream is certain, and the interpretation thereof sure.

That "*stone cut without hands*" is a different way to describe the same truth; that this One who will defeat the Devil, this One who will conquer the kingdoms of this world - is not the seed of a man.

Then the Prophet Isaiah, speaking about this very same truth says

Isaiah 7:14 KJV

Therefore the Lord himself shall give you a sign; Behold, a virgin shall conceive, and bear a son, and shall call his name Immanuel.

Indeed, this is exactly what happened

Luke 1:26-27 KJV
And in the sixth month the angel Gabriel was sent from God unto a city of Galilee, named Nazareth,
To a virgin espoused to a man whose name was Joseph, of the house of David; and the virgin's name was Mary.

Luke 1:30-35 KJV
And the angel said unto her, Fear not, Mary: for thou hast found favour with God.
And, behold, thou shalt conceive in thy womb, and bring forth a son, and shalt call his name JESUS.
He shall be great, and shall be called the Son of the Highest: and the Lord God shall give unto him the throne of his father David:
And he shall reign over the house of Jacob for ever; and of his kingdom there shall be no end.
Then said Mary unto the angel, How shall this be, seeing I know not a man?
And the angel answered and said unto her, The Holy Ghost shall come upon thee, and the power of the Highest shall overshadow thee: therefore also that holy thing which shall be born of thee shall be called the Son of God.

Two things separate the faith of Christians from that of every other religion:

- **No other faith was founded by the very Son of God and**
- **No other faith was founded by One who rose from the Dead**

Christianity, true Christianity, is unlike any religion in the world.

- **Ours is not based on the ideas of men**
- **Ours comes directly from God, who became man and dwelt among us.**

In Christ's baptism I see Jesus'
RELATIONSHIP THROUGH IDENTITY
Matthew 3:17 KJV
And lo a voice from heaven, saying, This is my beloved Son, in whom I am well pleased.

I am now focusing on that word, "**My.**" God the Father identified with Jesus and said, "He is *MY* beloved Son". Jesus is the Son of God through the virgin birth - He was not conceived at the time of His birth but has existed forever with the Father.

And then Jesus is God the Son through His very being. Jesus once said
"I am my Father are one"[47]

Many years ago there was a man who challenged me that Jesus was not really God. My oldest son, Bohannan, had just been born and this guy claimed that Jesus was merely a look alike to God just as Bohannan might look like me and even have my DNA, but he would never be me,

But that is not what the Bible says.
In a manner that we will never fully understand in this life and will probably spend all of eternity coming to understand in the next, Jesus is not only the express image of God, He is very God.

When the Apostle Philip asked Jesus to show them the Father Jesus answered
John 14:9 KJV
Jesus saith unto him, Have I been so long time with you, and yet hast thou not known me, Philip? he that hath seen me hath seen the Father; and how sayest thou then, Shew us the Father?

Later on, the Apostle Paul wrote of Jesus Christ
Philippians 2:6 KJV
Who, being in the form of God, thought it not robbery to be equal with God:

One commentary writes,

_____

[47] John 10:30

"in the form of God, imports not Christ's appearance in exerting of God's power, but his real and actual existence in the Divine essence."[48]

He not only looks like God, but He is the real and actual existence of God.

In a passage I preached from not to long ago, the Apostle John wrote
1 John 5:7 KJV
For there are three that bear record in heaven, the Father, the Word, and the Holy Ghost: and these three are one.

- **Jesus has an *eternal* relationship with His Heavenly Father as His beloved Son and**
- **Jesus has an *essential* relationship with His Heavenly Father as they are one and the same God**

I see in Christ's baptism Jesus'
RELATIONSHIP THROUGH SYMPATHY
Matthew 3:14-15 KJV
But John forbad him, saying, I have need to be baptized of thee, and comest thou to me?
And Jesus answering said unto him, Suffer it to be so now: for thus it becometh us to fulfil all righteousness. Then he suffered him.

Jesus did not have to be baptized to go to heaven.
- **He is God in the flesh**
- **He makes the rules, He does not have to follow the rules**

But Jesus submitted to baptism because, *it becometh us to fulfil all righteousness.*
- **Equal with God**
- **The express image of God and**
- **Favored by God**
Yet Jesus still chose to submit Himself to God.

---

[48] COMMENTARY by Matthew Poole, accessed through E-sword

There is a lesson here for all the carefree Christians who feel like since they are saved by grace they can run free with their lives.. Just because you do not have to obey God is no good reason to disobey God.

The book of Hebrews says that Jesus attitude was
Hebrews 10:9 KJV
.... Lo, I come to do thy will, O God. ...

Would to God we would see more Christian pick up that attitude. Instead of seeing what we can get away with, why don't we see what God might do with us, if we ever fully surrendered our wills to do God's will.

Jesus said,
John 4:34 KJV
... My meat is to do the will of him that sent me, and to finish his work.

John 6:38 KJV
For I came down from heaven, not to do mine own will, but the will of him that sent me.

- **Jesus came to do the will of His Heavenly Father but more**
- **Jesus finished the will of His Heavenly Father**

John 17:1-4 KJV
These words spake Jesus, and lifted up his eyes to heaven, and said, Father, ...
I have glorified thee on the earth: I have finished the work which thou gavest me to do.

In Philippians 2:5-8 KJV the Bible says
Let this mind be in you, which was also in Christ Jesus:
Who, being in the form of God, thought it not robbery to be equal with God:
But made himself of no reputation, and took upon him the form of a servant, and was made in the likeness of men:

And being found in fashion as a man, he humbled himself, and became obedient unto death, even the death of the cross.

God sent
- **His Son**
- **His beloved Son**
- **His only begotten Son**

to die on the cross, not for His own sins for He had none. He died for your sins and mine.

Jesus obeyed His Heavenly Father because He loved you and me so much that His Father willingly gave His Son and Jesus willingly gave His own life so that my sins and yours could be forgiven, forgotten and removed forever from the pages of God's record.

Have you come to Jesus so that your sins might be forgiven? Are you secure in your faith that you are not just religious, but that your sins are forgotten?

Christian - I am not asking you to pretend to be God, but I am asking you to follow the example of Christ.

Philippians 2:5-8 KJV
Let this mind be in you, which was also in Christ Jesus:
.... who made himself of no reputation, and took upon Himself the form of a servant....and became obedient...

Will you ask God to give you that mind?

Chapter Nineteen

The Confession of Christ

John 14:1-6 KJV

Let not your heart be troubled: ye believe in God, believe also in me.
In my Father's house are many mansions: if it were not so, I would
have told you. I go to prepare a place for you.
And if I go and prepare a place for you, I will come again, and receive
you unto myself; that where I am, there ye may be also.
And whither I go ye know, and the way ye know.
Thomas saith unto him, Lord, we know not whither thou goest; and
how can we know the way?
Jesus saith unto him, I am the way, the truth, and the life: no man
cometh unto the Father, but by me.

When we hear the word confession, we most often think of
someone making an admission of guilt.

- **A crook confesses to a crime**
- **A Catholic confesses to the priest**
- **A Christian confesses to the Lord**

1 John 1:9

If we confess our sins He is faithful and just to forgive us our sins and
to cleanse us from all unrighteousness

But that isn't the only way the word may be used. It can be
used to mean an affirmation of truth.

Years ago, a statement of Christian faith would have been
called a confession:

- **The Presbyterians had their Westminster Confession in 1646**
- **The Baptists of London produced their own confession of**
  faith in 1641 and revised it in 1689 to be much more like the
  Westminster
- **The Baptists of America produced the Philadelphia**
  Confession of Faith in 1742

Many times, before a Christian was martyred for their faith,
they would write out their confession – those things which

they believed and for which they were dying. And they would do this in accord with the pattern of the Apostle Paul who, when tried for his faith testified:

Acts 24:14-17 KJV

But this I confess unto thee, that after the way which they call heresy, so worship I the God of my fathers, believing all things which are written in the law and in the prophets:

And have hope toward God, which they themselves also allow, that there shall be a resurrection of the dead, both of the just and unjust.

And herein do I exercise myself, to have always a conscience void of offence toward God, and toward men.

Now after many years I came to bring alms to my nation, and offerings.

I want to submit to you that the Lord Jesus Christ made His own confession of faith and that it is recorded in this passage of the events of the day previous to His Crucifixion. That Confession is,

John 14:6 KJV

Jesus saith unto him, I am the way, the truth, and the life: no man cometh unto the Father, but by me.

A POSITIVE STATEMENT

Jesus saith unto him, I am

We use the phrase " I am" pretty casually don't we?

- **I am *so* hungry**
- **I am *so* hot**
- **"I am the greatest"[49]**

Sometimes we say we are hungry but what we really mean is that we want to eat.

- **We haven't gone without food**
- **We aren't to the point of starving**

We just aren't used to going very long without having something to chew on. It's a casual statement.

But when Jesus said "I am" it takes on a whole new quality.

---

[49] Mohammed Ali's famous sentiment about himself.

With those words, we are taken clear back to about 1450 BC, when Moses spoke with God at the burning bush.

God told Moses that he wanted him to return to Egypt from the dessert where he had lived for the last 40 years, and to lead the children of Israel out of Egyptian slavery. Moses was naturally concerned.

- **What would compel Pharaoh to let them go? and**
- **Why would the Israelites want to go with him?**

So Moses asked God,
Exodus 3:13 KJV
... when I come unto the children of Israel, and shall say unto them, The God of your fathers hath sent me unto you; and they shall say to me, What is his name? what shall I say unto them?

And to this question God replied,
Exodus 3:14 KJV
...., I AM THAT I AM: and he said, Thus shalt thou say unto the children of Israel, I AM hath sent me unto you.

Whenever Jesus used that phrase, we ought to read into it the name of God.

- **I am... the bread of life[50]**
- **I am ....meek and lowly of heart[51]**
- **I am ... with you alway[52]**
- **I am ... come in my Father's name[53]**
- **I am ... the light of the world[54]**
- **I am... not alone[55]**
- **I am...from above[56]**
- **I am ...the door[57]**

---

[50] John 6:35
[51] Matthew 11:29
[52] Matthew 28:20
[53] John 5:43
[54] John 8:12
[55] John 8:16
[56] John 8:23

- **I am …the good shepherd**[58]
- **I am … the vine**[59]
- **I am … the Son of God**[60]
- **I am …the resurrection and the life**[61]

Do you see what I mean?

This are very positive statements regarding His relationship
- **With God**
- **With heaven and**
- **With our salvation**

"Moses, all you need to know is my name is 'I am.'"

A DEFINITIVE STATEMENT
the way, the truth, and the life

We are given here three simple, but profoundly powerful statements

A. The way
That means more than He knows the way, He is the way.

Jesus said in John 10:9
I am the door: by me if any man enter in he shall be saved and shall go in and out and find pasture."

He is the way to the Father, to heaven.

We cannot come to the Father
- **By our church or**
- **By our religious deeds, or**
- **By what we think to be right**

---

[57] John 10:9
[58] John 10:11
[59] John 15:5
[60] John 10:36
[61] John 11:25

We can only come to the Father's house by Jesus Christ.

He
- **Takes care of our passport**
- **Signs all the documents and**
- **Makes all the payments**

We just leave it up to Him and trust Him that He is able.

B. The truth
Truth is a very narrow-minded thing. Something is either truth or it is a lie. This means our opinions about how to go to heaven don't matter. Jesus said, *"I am the truth, and I am the only way to the Father's house."*

Truth is very intolerant of error. Have you ever made an error in your check book which cost you money? Once that error is made, you can
- **Smile a lot**
- **Beg**
- **Plead**
- **Be good, and**
- **Take your banker out to dinner**

But you still pay for the error.

If a person does not come by Jesus it does not matter
- **How good they have been**
- **How much money they have given to church**
- **How many times they have been baptized or**
- **How much they plead**

The truth of the matter is, there is no way to get to heaven but by Jesus.

That is what Jesus said.

C. The Life
That means He is the source of life.

You live today because Jesus wills it.
- **He breathed the breath of life in all of us.**
- **He holds our lives in His hands**
- **He created us.**[62]

He is,
1. Eternal life
All of us who are in Christ shall never die. Physical death will only serve to usher us into another realm, but we will live eternally.

Jesus is also,
2. Abundant life
You want to know how to get the very most out of life? Exchange yours for Christ's. Let your life be hid in Jesus and let His life be lived through you.

The happiest a person can ever be, I believe, is knowing they are doing what Jesus would do if He were in their place. Letting Jesus live through you doesn't mean that everything will always go your way. But there is no greater joy than seeing God's will done on this earth.

And that starts when God's will is done in you and me.

AN EXCLUSIVE STATEMENT
no man cometh unto the Father, but by me.

We don't like this phrase very much in our world these days.
- **We like tolerance**
- **We like acceptance**
- **We like "come as you are" thinking**

---

[62] Revelation 4:11
And for His pleasure we are and were created

And it is just not how Jesus dealt with things.

- **There are those who will say that Paul was like he was because of his culture**
- **There are those who say that Bible can be interpreted different ways for different times**

But this is Jesus Christ. He is either God or He is a liar.

And Jesus Christ said,
…no man cometh unto the Father but by me."

- *"No man"* **is the hero who gives his life for his country but does not know Jesus as Saviour**
- *"No man"* **is the daddy who loved his kids wholeheartedly, but never came to know Christ as Saviour**
- *"No man"* **is the philanthropist who gives away a fortune to help the unfortunate but is not a believer in Jesus Christ alone**
- *"No man"* **is the momma, who sacrifices everything to see that her kids are well kept and brought up, but is not saved**

- *"No man"* **is the pastor who has preached 10,000 sermons in his lifetime, but never knelt at the cross and asked Jesus to save him**
- *"No man"* **is the deacon who has helped a hundred souls to find peace in Jesus Christ, but never came to that peace himself**

- *"No man"* **is the Mormon who earnestly keeps his religion, but does not know the saving power of Christ**
- *"No man"* **is the Jehovah's Witness who has visited hundred of houses distributing their literature but has mistaken Jesus for a lesser god**
- *"No man"* **is the Catholic, who has gone to mass faithfully, but has not come to Jesus**

- *"No man"* **is the Muslim who believes Jesus to be a prophet, but does not know Him as the Son of God**

"No man" means that
- **Every other way**
- **Every other truth and**

- **Every other life**

Is
- **False**
- **Error**
- **Heresy**
- **Mistaken**
- **Wrong**

"No man" is a personal thing. It brings it right down to my territory and to yours.

Jesus did not say,
- **No country**
- **No religion**
- **No ethnic background**
- **No organization**

If He had done that, I might have been able to hide myself somewhere in the masses.

But He said,
No man cometh unto the Father but by me

So that means
- **No man**
- **No woman**
- **No boy**
- **No girl**
- **No aunt**
- **No uncle**
- **No mom**
- **No dad**
- **No brother**
- **No sister**

Right away two things become urgent in my mind: The first is, **What about me?** If no man can come to the Father but by Jesus Christ – I need to make sure I have come to Jesus

Christ. The tendency is to ignore and brush this aside. No one wants to think about death and dying and especially if there is a chance that hell is where we would go. But there is no better time than right now and no better place than right here to confront these things head on and come to a solution.

- **This is a place designed by God to give souls true hope for salvation**
- **This is the time ordained by the Lord for you to hear a clear message of heaven and hell.**

So

- **This is the perfect hour for you settle where you will spend all eternity**

The second urgency is, **What about everyone else?** It is a sorry man who finds a well of water and won't share it with the thirsty. How could you possibly be saved and willingly withhold that from a lost man?

I know the argument; "They don't want to hear?"

I have ten adorable puppies at home right now.
They are just about ready to be weaned and begin eating solid food. But the process is a time consuming one for me.

- **First, I have to prepare this "gruel" out of dog food**
- **Then I have to stick each puppy's nose in the food and coax it to eat**

They don't like me pushing their nose in the food. They don't like the taste of the food right now. And there are ten of them that,

- **Push against me when I put their nose in the plate**
- **Scratch at me to stop me from doing it**
- **Cry because I am doing it and**
- **Refuse to eat even though I did it for their own good**

So what do you think? Should I just give up? Their mom won't let them eat her milk much longer. As soon as they have those needle-sharp teeth, she's not fixing dinner anymore! No. The only right thing to do is to gently, lovingly, persistently keep taking them to the food until they get it.

And that's exactly what we need to do with the gospel.
We can't force people to be saved. But we can,
- **Keep praying for them**
- **Keep being kind to them**
- **Keep witnessing to them**
- **Keep inviting them**
- **Keep encouraging them**

And some of them, will come to the Father by Jesus Christ.

Chapter Twenty
NO GREAT CONTROVERSY
1 Timothy 3:16

There are, in this world, many controversies that may never be resolved:
- **The opinions of conservatives versus liberals**
- **The ideas of capitalists versus socialists**
- **The battle between Creationists and the Evolutionists**

Conflicts between **democracies** and **tyrannies** will no doubt continue so long as one man longs to rule and the common people long for freedom. Controversies are such a part of human life that one guy said, "If you get two Baptist preachers together to express their views on a subject, you will end up with three opinions!"

Spiritually there are controversies that rage over,
- **Calvinism vs Arminianism**
- **Legalism vs Liberalism**
- **Conservativism vs Progressivism**
- **Fundamentalism vs Evagelicalism**
- **Lordship Salvation vs Easy Believism**
- **Pre Tribulationalism vs Mid Tribulationalism**
- **King James Version vs Any other version**
- **Immersion baptism vs Sprinkling baptism**
- **Baby baptism vs Adult baptism**
- **Contemporary Christian Music vs Old Fashioned Music**
- **Local church vs Universal church**
- **Pastoral leadership vs Congregational rule**

And I don't think I have even begun the list of those things that will not be settled until we get to heaven. (If all of us involved in these controversies are even saved and will go to heaven).

There are some great controversies in this world:
- **The debate over abortion**
- **The battle over same sex marriages**

- **The morality of stem cell research**

There have been controversies so great that men by the thousands have shed their blood and given their lives for them:
- **The controversy with England that led to our United States**
- **The controversy between the States that led to our strong Federal government and**
- **The controversy of WWII that led six million souls being slaughtered only just because they were Jews**

But I am here to tell you today that this one thing is no great controversy:
That what God claims to do in order that a soul would be forgiven of sin and go forever to heaven, the mystery of godliness, is indeed great.

- **You may not believe that it happened**
- **You might not believe that it is necessary**
- **You may be completely apathetic concerning the issue of salvation**

But what the Bible describes God doing in order to seek and to save the lost sinner is, without controversy, great.

Within this one verse is the gist of the entire New Testament Message.

God was,
MANIFEST IN THE FLESH
1 John 3:8 KJV
… For this purpose the Son of God was manifested, that he might destroy the works of the devil.

That God became flesh is the central theme of the entire Bible.

- **It begins with a promise in Genesis 3:15 that the seed of the woman would bruise the head of the seed of the serpent**
- **It is prophesied throughout the Old Testament**
- **It is fulfilled in the person of Jesus Christ**

Believe it or reject it; the idea that an infinite God would be personally united with a finite nature is a mystery greater than a mind can grasp.

There is the physics of the problem:
How can the God who is bigger than the universe possibly fit into the body of "pip-squeak human"?

Then there is the theology of the problem:
Why would God want to do such a thing?

- **We know our sin nature**
- **We know how hard this world can be**
- **We know about hunger, sweat, laziness, crime, disease, discouragement**

Why would God WANT to become a part of that? The answer is found in 1 John 3:8 KJV
... For this purpose the Son of God was manifested, that he might destroy the works of the devil.

He did it that He might destroy those very reasons why we wouldn't think He would want to come.

God was,
JUSTIFIED IN THE SPIRIT
Matthew 3:16 KJV
And Jesus, when he was baptized, went up straightway out of the water: and, lo, the heavens were opened unto him, and he saw the Spirit of God descending like a dove, and lighting upon him:

All this means is that the Holy Spirit tells us that Jesus is exactly who He said He was.

- **The Holy Spirit convinces us that Jesus is the Son of God**
- **The Holy Spirit convinces us that Jesus is the Saviour of the world**
- **The Holy Spirit convinces us that if we would call upon Jesus, He would forgive our sin**

John 16:7-11 KJV
Nevertheless I tell you the truth; It is expedient for you that I go away: for if I go not away, the Comforter will not come unto you; but if I depart, I will send him unto you.
And when he is come, he will reprove the world of sin, and of righteousness, and of judgment:
Of sin, because they believe not on me;
Of righteousness, because I go to my Father, and ye see me no more;
Of judgment, because the prince of this world is judged.

Everything we believe about Jesus Christ is
- **Written in this Bible and**
- **Confirmed by the conviction of the Holy Spirit in our hearts**

This work of the Holy Spirit is necessary because no sinful man would ever believe this "mystery of godliness" without it.

If you are saved right now it is
- **Not because you were brought up that way**
- **Not because you had a bent toward the spiritual**
- **Not because a Sunday school teacher told you how to be saved**
- **Not because you have always believed in Jesus**

But you are saved because the Holy Spirit of God confirmed to your heart the truth that Jesus Christ is God, made flesh to save you from your sins.

God was,
SEEN OF ANGELS
Hebrews 1:6 KJV
And again, when he bringeth in the firstbegotten into the world, he saith, And let all the angels of God worship him.

Of course, He was.

- **He created the angels and**
- **He has forever lived in heaven where the angels are**

The context of this tells us that He was seen of the angels while He was on the earth. We know that,

- **Angels ministered to Him after he was tempted by the devil in the wilderness and that**
- **Angels strengthened Him while He was praying in the Garden of Gethsemane**

The suggestion is that this mystery of godliness is so great that it excites the interests of the angels of heaven.

1 Peter 1:12 KJV

Unto whom it was revealed, that not unto themselves, but unto us they did minister the things, which are now reported unto you by them that have preached the gospel unto you with the Holy Ghost sent down from heaven; which things the angels desire to look into.

The work of Jesus Christ might be boring to the majority of people, but it is a fascinating subject to the inhabitants of glory.

God was

PREACHED UNTO THE GENTILES

Colossians 1:26-27 KJV

Even the mystery which hath been hid from ages and from generations, but now is made manifest to his saints:
To whom God would make known what is the riches of the glory of this mystery among the Gentiles; which is Christ in you, the hope of glory:

I like how Barnes Notes puts this. He says, "The [mystery of godliness[63]] ... was adapted "to man" as such - without regard to his

- **Complexion,**
- **Country,**

---

[63] My words

- **Customs, or**
- **Laws"**

One of the greatest features of this great "mystery of godliness" is that no one is excluded. Anyone can be saved. Anyone can be made godly in the sight of God

- **It doesn't matter your background**
- **It doesn't matter the nature of your past sins**
- **It doesn't matter what others have thought about you**

God sees you differently than any human being you have ever known has looked at you.

- **He sees you as the object of His love**
- **He sees you as a potential of His salvation**
- **He sees you and either having accepted Christ or needing to accept Christ.**

If you have not trusted Christ as Saviour
He only sees your need

If you have trusted Christ as Saviour
He only sees Christ in you as your hope of glory

God was,

BELIEVED ON IN THE WORLD
Acts 17:6 KJV
And when they found them not, they drew Jason and certain brethren unto the rulers of the city, crying, These that have turned the world upside down are come hither also;

One of the greatest parts of this mystery is that people from all over the world have believed on Jesus Christ as Saviour:

- **Orientals**
- **Asians**
- **Island People**
- **Europeans**
- **East Indians and**
- **American Indians**

Anywhere the gospel has been preached there have been people who willingly and anxiously believe upon Him as their own Saviour.

This despite:
- **That the message is of Christ is so great as to be unbelievable without the confirmation of the Holy Spirit and**
- **That men seem so bent toward not believing such a fantastic message**

Furthermore, this mystery of godliness has "been embraced, not by a few, but by thousands in all lands….."[64]

God was,

RECEIVED UP INTO GLORY
Acts 1:9-11 KJV
And when he had spoken these things, while they beheld, he was taken up; and a cloud received him out of their sight.
And while they looked stedfastly toward heaven as he went up, behold, two men stood by them in white apparel;
Which also said, Ye men of Galilee, why stand ye gazing up into heaven? this same Jesus, which is taken up from you into heaven, shall so come in like manner as ye have seen him go into heaven.

In this phrase is incorporated
- **His resurrection,**
- **His ascension into heaven and also**
- **His eventual return to this earth**

Can you imagine being one of those disciples as Jesus began to lift from off the earth and gradually rise higher and higher until he was no longer visible? No wonder they stood their gazing up into heaven!

I think of another passage which says
"*We never saw it on this fashion.*"[65]

---

[64] Albert Barnes' Notes on the Bible, Albert Barnes (1798-1870)

- **They had watched Christ turn water into wine**
- **They had seen Him walk on water and calm raging seas**
- **They had seen him heal the sick, make the blind see and the lame walk**
- **They had even seen him raise people from the dead**

But this was a brand new thing.

Elijah, they had read, rode the chariot of God into heaven. But Jesus didn't even need the chariot. And then comes these angels, *Which also said, Ye men of Galilee, why stand ye gazing up into heaven? this same Jesus, which is taken up from you into heaven, shall so come in like manner as ye have seen him go into heaven.*

None of us will ever see Christ rise to heaven as they did. But all of us who are saved will witness when He comes again "...*in like manner as ye have seen Him go into heaven."*

Do what you will with the story of Christ; anyone must admit that the story is a great one.

Great in its scope

Covering everyone from the beginning of time to the end of time

Great in its imagery

That God became man and dwelt among us

But mostly this mystery is,

Great in its potential

All who will come to Jesus Christ, Jesus said, He would in no wise cast out.

- **You can be saved**
- **You can be forgiven your sins**
- **You can have a real fellowship with God**

---

[65] Mark 2:12

- **You can know for sure you will go to heaven and**
- **You can live the rest of your days – not just muddling by until you are gone, but with purpose and meaning and joy beyond imagination**

Fundamentals Concerning Church

Chapter Twenty-One
THIS IS THE PLACE
1 Timothy 3:1-16

Some friends went to dinner with us and, during our conversation, they mentioned that many if not most of their friends, who grew up in a Fundamental Baptist Church have left fundamental churches to either not attend church or to go to very progressive churches. We were discussing some of the reasons for that. I am not sure I know all of the answers but I have a few theories, one of them being that a lot of preaching during the 60's and 70's on through the 80's and 90's and still remains today, focused on applications from the Bible rather than the Bible itself. The preaching was about does and don'ts. I liken to very old-fashioned Methodist mentality.

- **Get people saved**
- **Then give them a set of "methods" to live by**

I think the intention was honest and just, they were trying to give people tools

- **To honor God with their lives**
- **To win souls to the Saviour**
- **To influence the course of our country**
- **To raise kids that were immune from worldiness**
- **To build churches that were lighthouses for Christ**

but what was left out was, if I may put it fairly bluntly, the Bible. Scriptures were read as support texts – but people were left to figure out the passage for themselves.

- **What the first readers of the Bible would have learned from the Bible**
- **What the writers were originally addressing and**
- **What the basic doctrines that they were teaching**

were left untouched from the pulpit, or sometimes just barely touched.

I think what happened was that those preachers, as long as they worked hard and were dynamic enough leaders, were able to keep a band of people together,

- **On the hope that their kids would turn out**
- **On the promise that our country would turn around and**
- **On the sheer energy of the crowds that they assembled**

but eventually the energy wore out, the kids didn't always turn out and our country has done far from turning around. Those people who grew up under those hopes, have become disillusioned and have either quit church altogether or gone to a church very different than the one that promised them all of those things.

This book is meant to give us the grounding of solid doctrines – found right from the Bible.

We have looked to see

- **What the Bible says about God**
- **What the Bible says about the Bible**
- **What the Bible says about heaven and hell**
- **What the Bible says about Jesus Christ**

For the next few chapters, I want to look to see what the Bible says about the church.

I am not sure most Christians today would think of the church as a "fundamental, basic" doctrine. I think that almost every Christian has bought into some form of the idea that church doesn't really matter.

- **Church is a place to find friends**
- **Church is a place to get a third-rate kind of entertainment**
- **Church is a place where we come to give God our offerings to Him**

In other words, church is sort of an optional extra for the Christian.

I hope to point out to you that God's view of the Church is much higher than that.

Notice 1 Timothy 3:15 KJV
But if I tarry long, that thou mayest know how thou oughtest to behave thyself in the house of God, which is the church of the living God, the pillar and ground of the truth.

It is interesting where we find this verse placed in the Bible; it is sandwiched between
A. The qualifications for the only two offices the Bible allows for a local church
- **The bishop, (or Pastor)**
- **The deacon**

B. The single most definitive verse in all the Bible concerning Jesus Christ

That tells me two things:
First, the church the verse addresses is a local congregation, not an invisible body of believers
Second, that it rests itself upon the doctrines of Jesus Christ

- **Its *function* is through the offices of pastor and deacon and**
- **Its *purpose* is to ground people on the doctrines of Jesus Christ**

Speaking of ground; notice the three titles given for this church
- **The house of God**
- **The church of the living God and**
- **The pillar and ground of the truth**

Ground always has a specific location. I am buying a house that sits on a piece of ground having a particular longitude and latitude.
- **It never moves.**
- **It never shifts a little**
- **It never occupies a different longitude and latitude than it had when I first bought it.**

Years ago I read a book by Samuel Clemens entitled "Roughing It". It's the story of his first journey away from his home on the Mississippi. His brother had been appointed as the secretary of the Nevada territory and he went as his brother's aide.

He tells the story of a certain farmer who took a neighbor to court for his farm. Clemens says that the one farmer's property was on a hill just above this other farmer's property. During a really bad rain, the one farmer's land slid off the hill and all of his topsoil ended up on his neighbor's property. He lost the court case. But that's about the only time I have ever heard of anyone thinking his land really did change longitude and latitude.

Ground stays in one place. Putting a pillar on that ground means the pillar stays too.

The Greeks built their Parthenon in Athens in about the year 450 BC. Over the last 2500 years a lot of things have changed in Athens
- **The Greeks were overrun by the Romans**
- **The Romans were overrun by the Ostrogoths**
- **The Ostrogoths were overrun by the Ottomans**

Eventually Greece became its own country again.

The Parthenon was pillaged and plundered. It has decayed over time. But one thing hasn't changed; the original location of those pillars.

God's Word says of the House of God, which is the church of the living God, that it is *the pillar and the ground of the truth*.

I want to try to build for you four pillars on that piece of ground that God says is the church of the living God.

The church is,
THE PLACE OF TRUTH

People have all sorts of different ideas where truth is to be found; I am here to tell you where truth is not to be found:

A. You will never find truth in the world of academics
2 Timothy 3:1-7 KJV
This know also, that in the last days perilous times shall come.
For men shall be lovers of their own selves, covetous, boasters, proud, blasphemers, disobedient to parents, unthankful, unholy,
Without natural affection, trucebreakers, false accusers, incontinent, fierce, despisers of those that are good,
Traitors, heady, highminded, lovers of pleasures more than lovers of God;
Having a form of godliness, but denying the power thereof: from such turn away.
For of this sort are they which creep into houses, and lead captive silly women laden with sins, led away with divers lusts,
Ever learning, and never able to come to the knowledge of the truth.

It doesn't take a whole lot of listening to the professors and teachers in the schools of higher education to figure out that the one thing they all know is that they don't know anything.

- **Archeologists and**
- **Historians**
- **Anthropologists and**
- **Physicists**

All have this one thing in common; they are ever learning, but never able to come to the knowledge of the truth. In fact, the least academic thing a professor can say is *"I know…"* The best they ever can do is to say, *"We believe…"*

I think their biggest complaint about Christianity is that Christians say we know certain things to be true. They would be willing to debate with Christians, I think, except that we would never yield to the idea that the Bible is just a theory.

Further
B. You will never find truth in the world of science
1 Timothy 6:20 KJV
O Timothy, keep that which is committed to thy trust, avoiding profane and vain babblings, and oppositions of science falsely so called:

Science could be true because science is supposed to be the discovery of knowledge.

Proverbs 25:2 KJV
It is the glory of God to conceal a thing: but the honour of kings is to search out a matter.

That's science; begin with the simple idea that God has created order in the universe and given us the blessing of discovering it.

But today's science, just like Paul's day, is "science - falsely so called." It starts from the premise that the first truth is "there is no God." and then sets out to prove it. So much so that many scientists, who are believers, are being blackballed is disbarred from their fields.

C. You will never find truth in the world of philosophy
Colossians 2:8 KJV
Beware lest any man spoil you through philosophy and vain deceit, after the tradition of men, after the rudiments of the world, and not after Christ.

The word philosophy literally means "the love of wisdom." But since the days of Socrates, it has been the wisdom of man and not of God.

There is only one place where truth can be found, that is, *"...in the house of God, the church of the living God the pillar and ground of the truth."*

Now I would like to expand slightly upon that and suggest the church is also

THE PLACE OF FAITH

Paul was writing to the church of the Thessalonians when he said, 1 Thessalonians 1:8 KJV

For from you sounded out the word of the Lord not only in Macedonia and Achaia, but also in every place your faith to God-ward is spread abroad; so that we need not to speak any thing.

The word faith means a persuasion or conviction, especially about religious truth. Not only is the church a place to find truth, it is a place to embrace it, to become persuaded and convicted by it. The church is the place where truth takes hold of us and makes us different creatures than we once were.

The church is not supposed to be,
- **The place where we enjoy our friends**
- **The place where we work to relieve world suffering**
- **The place where we meet our future mates**

Those all might happen at church.

But the church is to be the place where,
- **We hear the truth of God's Word**
- **We allow it to dig deep into our hearts and**
- **We begin to take on the shape of that truth in daily living**

If the church is the ground of the truth, then I am confident that I am not stretching the Word to say it is also

THE PLACE OF CHRIST

Jesus said

John 14:6 KJV

... I am the way, the truth, and the life: no man cometh unto the Father, but by me.

People think all sorts of things are true.
- **Some people think it is true that the earth was formed by a gigantic explosion**

- Some people think it is true that mankind evolved from apes who evolved from fish who evolved from germs who got zapped to life by the big bang
- Some people think it is true that there is no God

I am here to say that there is only one absolute truth. He is Jesus Christ.

There may be truth in some other things
- It is true that electricity can turn on lights
- It is true that gasoline can burn in a combustion engine
- It is true that a resting healthy heart beats 70 or so times a minute

But none of that is truth:
- The truth that set a soul free from sin
- The truth that opens the way to the Heavenly Father
- The truth that sanctifies and sets us apart for God's purposes

Jesus Christ is the truth and since the church is the pillar and the ground of the truth, can you guess where it is you will find Christ?

- He isn't up in the mountains
- He isn't out at your favorite lake
- He isn't at some secluded spot on the beach

Jesus Christ resides right here; – the house of God, which is the church of the living God.

And that leads me to one last point.
- The church is the place of truth
- The church is the place of faith
- The church is the place of Christ

So, the church ought to be,
THE PLACE OF THE CHRISTIAN
Hebrews 10:24-25 KJV

And let us consider one another to provoke unto love and to good works:
Not forsaking the assembling of ourselves together, as the manner of some is; but exhorting one another: and so much the more, as ye see the day approaching.

Allow me to make a rather bold statement. To say that you believe in God you don't believe in organized religion is deny the God who is revealed in the Bible. This God assembles His people

- **From Noah calling his sons into the ark**
- **To Moses organizing the twelve tribes around the tabernacle**
- **To Paul urge us not to forsake the assembling of ourselves together**
- **To Jesus gathering all of the believers to himself in the clouds**

- **Every Christian ought to be a part of a local church**
- **Every Christian ought to be faithful to the services of that church and**
- **Every Christian ought to serve God in that church and by bringing people to that church**

Chapter Twenty-Two
CHRIST AND THE CHURCH
Ephesians 5:22-32

This is one of our favorite passages to use
- **In preparing couples for**
- **In counseling couples after marriage and**
- **In a message delivered during a wedding ceremony**

- **Preachers refer to it often in preaching on the family and the home**
- **Husbands will use it frequently, when they want to get their wives to follow them**

And the passage is good for all of that.

But there is an interesting phrase found in the passage that we seldom spend any time meditating upon. Ephesians 5:32 says of this passage
"This is a great mystery, but I speak of Christ and the church."

In other words, the Bible says,
- **"I know this is a difficult concept**
- **I know this is a little more tough to grab hold of**
- **I know that this is more on the fuzzy side of your mind**

But I am not talking about husbands and wives primarily; they are the shadow of the truth.
- **The body,**
- **The larger subject,**
- **The more important message here is**

"Christ and the church"

How many of us, who have read this passage with any kind of frequency, have not done something like this, We read the passage and in our minds eye, we make bold the words having to do with people, and we let the words having to do with Christ and the church sort of zoom out of focus.

Ephesians 5:22-25

Wives, submit yourselves unto your own husbands, *as unto the Lord.*

For the husband is the head of the wife, *even as Christ is the head of the church: and he is the saviour of the body.*

Therefore as the church is subject unto Christ, **so let the wives be to their own husbands in every thing.**

Husbands, love your wives, *even as Christ also loved the church, and gave himself for it;* (KJV)

We tend to think of Christ and His relationship to the church as an illustration of what marriage ought to be like. But that is exactly the opposite as the emphasis the Bible places on it. God's word uses the marriage relationship as an illustration of Christ's relationship to his church

There is no greater love story in all of the world than is the love story between Christ and the church. When God looked down upon Adam and said *"it is not good that man should be alone."* He caused a deep sleep to fall upon Adam and God took one of Adam's ribs and made woman from it. Adam looked at Eve and said *"this is now bone of my bones and flesh of my flesh."*

The beauty of that picture is found in how it represents *Christ and the church.*

When Isaac was 40 years old and ready to have a wife Abraham sent his servant back to Abraham's family to find a bride for his son. Rebekah willingly,
- **Left all she had ever known**
- **To travel with a virtual stranger**
- **To a land she had never seen**
- **To marry a man she had only days ago even heard of**

The Bible says,
Genesis 24:63-67

And Isaac went out to meditate in the field at the eventide: and he lifted up his eyes, and saw, and, behold, the camels were coming.
And Rebekah lifted up her eyes, and when she saw Isaac, she lighted off the camel.
For she had said unto the servant, What man is this that walketh in the field to meet us? And the servant had said, It is my master: therefore she took a vail, and covered herself.
….
And Isaac brought her into his mother Sarah's tent, and took Rebekah, and she became his wife; and he loved her: …. (KJV)

The beauty of this love story is in how it represents *Christ and the church.*

When Jacob spotted Rachel tending to her father's sheep the Bible makes it clear that Jacob fell in love with her at first sight. Jacob approached her father, asking for her hand in marriage, and the deal was made that Jacob would serve Laban seven years before he could marry his daughter. And the Bible says,
Genesis 29:20
And Jacob served seven years for Rachel; and they seemed unto him but a few days, for the love he had to her. (KJV)

The wonder of that statement is in how it represents *Christ and the church*

- **Ruth and Boaz**
- **David and Michal**
- **Esther and Ahasuerus**
- **Solomon and the Shunamite**

Every great love story in the Word of God is recorded for how it represents *Christ and the church.*

And may I say that each and every great marriage we are able to witness in our lifetimes, are beautiful to behold, most of all for how they portray *Christ and the Church*

- **Every loving glance between a husband and a wife**
- **Every tender touch of the hand**
- **Every kind word, softly spoken**

is wonderful to witness because it represents **Christ and the church**

There are at least three great truths in Ephesians 5 concerning Christ and the church.

Christ is
THE SOVEREIGN OF THE CHURCH
Vs 22-24

Jesus is the head of the church. Obviously it speaks of authority for the church is "*subject unto Christ.*" But there is so much more here than mere dictatorship over the church because He is the Saviour of the body (which is the church).

The head provides,
A. Function
Every body part works either voluntarily or involuntarily through the direction of the brain (head).

Jesus,
"upholds all things by the word of His power."

- **Every function of the church**
- **Every working part**
- **Every member of the church**

Comes to us through Jesus Christ the head.

- **Every accomplishment of the church**
- **Every achievement of the church**
- **Every good work of the church, either done purposefully or one that just happens**

All happens because Jesus ordered it so.

The head provides,

B. Education

The processes of thought all occur through the head. And that is exactly what Jesus does for His church. He has given to us everything we need to think about.

Even the Holy Spirit, the Bible says,
John 16:13
.... shall not speak of himself; but whatsoever he shall hear, that shall he speak: .... (KJV)

Jesus told us what things to think about in,
Philippians 4:8
Finally, brethren, whatsoever things are true, whatsoever things are honest, whatsoever things are just, whatsoever things are pure, whatsoever things are lovely, whatsoever things are of good report; if there be any virtue, and if there be any praise, think on these things. (KJV)

We are told how often to think about them in,
Psalms 1:2
But his delight is in the law of the LORD; and in his law doth he meditate day and night. (KJV)

And we are told,
Proverbs 19:27
Cease, my son, to hear the instruction that causeth to err from the words of knowledge. (KJV)

Jesus provides all that ought to occupy our minds all the time.

And then the head provides,
C. Direction

Both in the abstract and the concrete meanings of the word.

It is through our minds that we make either wise or wayward choices in what to do in life. We take the instruction we were provided and use that wisdom to guide our direction in long term and short-term choices. **It is through the eyes** that we have direction in the more concrete choices.

Several years ago now, one of our church members told me a story. They said years ago they were making an all-night road trip through the southern states. Just before daylight, he was so tired he could hardly keep his eyes open.

- **So he closed one eye – just to give it a rest.**
- **It felt so good, he closed them both for only a second.**

And he noticed he stayed straight in the road. He thought maybe he could close them just a moment or two longer and then a moment or two longer. And the next thing he knew he was driving off the road at 60 miles per hour. You just can't keep a car going the right direction with your eyes closed.

The Lord Jesus Christ gives function, education and direction to his church. He is the head, the sovereign of the church

THE SACRIFICE FOR THE CHURCH
Vs 2 Vs 25

There is a subtle difference between these two verses, but there are also some important similarities between them.

A. Differences
Vs 2 speaks of "us"
Vs 25 speaks of "the church"

Verse 2 refers to you and me as individual children of God
Verse 25 refers to you and me as we are members of the local church

Jesus is our Saviour individually. Nobody gets saved under a group policy. You are not saved,

- **Because you were born in America**

- **Because your parents have been good Christians**
- **Because your best friend and you went forward when you were kids**

A person gets saved,
- **Personally,**
- **Independently,**
- **Individually**

But it is not God's intention that we stay that way. Yes, Christ died for us as individuals. But He also gave Himself for us to be a part of His body, the local church.

B. Similarities
Notice that in both verses there is the same motivator and the same action.
- **Jesus is motivated out of love and**
- **Love moved Him to give Himself**

The Bible says Christ's sacrifice was a *"sweetsmelling savour"* to God. God the Father did not enjoy watching Jesus die.
- **He turned His back on Christ on the cross and**
- **He caused the sun to stop shining in the middle of the day to hide His horrific agony**

but He was so pleased with the results.

Can you imagine how much God must love us that He would consider the death of His only begotten Son for us a *"sweetsmelling savour"*?

Christ is the sovereign of the church
Christ is the sacrifice for the church

Christ is
THE SUPPLIER OF THE CHURCH
Vs 26-29

There are three phrases I want to point out in this portion of the text:

A. Sanctify and cleanse
Vs 26

This is a separating work.

When a young couple gets married there is a time of growing together. They must leave some old friends and change their relationships with some others.

It can be a tough time on the new marriage.
The old self wants to have all the benefits of marriage without any of the losses.

The old self wants everything to stay the same in the world around them and only add onto it this one new thing – marriage.

And it just doesn't work. A process has to happen as the couple learns how to live as one new flesh.

The same is true in the spiritual realm.
- **We get saved and**
- **We get baptized and**
- **We become members of this new body, which is Christ's**

There is a process of cleansing – as Christ removes us from the old sins and past lifestyle

Then there is this process of sanctifying – as Christ leads us into a life dedicated to the things of God

B. Nourisheth and cheristheth
Vs 29
- **The word nourish means to mature or build up**
- **The word cherish means to brood and warm up**

I think Anita and I have pretty much learned how to live together. Thirty-three years now, and our lives are so intertwined it is difficult to find where one's interests leave off and the others begins. You know what we do now? We nourish and cherish what we have. We build up and brood over our marriage

- **I have always loved Anita,**
- **I have always thought we had the perfect marriage**

But our relationship is so much warmer these days it than has ever been before.

While Jesus is *sanctifying and cleansing* His church, He is also *fanning the flames of love* so that we – who are part of His church may love Him more and more the longer we know Him.

C. Present it to Himself
Vs 27

The word present means "**to stand beside**."

In my mind I am picturing that moment in the wedding ceremony when the couple turn, standing side by side, to face the congregation and I am privileged to say the words, "Ladies and Gentlemen; may I present to you Mr. and Mrs......" And they walk out of the room to begin a new life together.

One of these days Jesus Christ will take His bride, the church, to His side. He will call us into the glory of his presence and we, as members of His church, will walk side by side into eternity.

Ephesians 5 ends by saying, Ephesians 5:33
Nevertheless let every one of you in particular so love his wife even as himself; and the wife see that she reverence her husband. (KJV)

There are some great lessons in the chapter for our marriages today. But let's never forget the bigger, grander, more wonderful message of Ephesians 5

...... I speak concerning Christ and the church. (KJV)

Chapter Twenty-Three
The Mission of the Local Church
Matthew 28:18-20

I believe with all my heart in the local New Testament Baptist Church. I believe it is the answer for almost every problem we can list tonight.

- **It is the answer for the drunk, more than AA**
- **It is the answer for the family, more than Planned Parenthood**
- **It is the answer for the country more than either the republicans or the democrats.**

- **The local church is the answer for a father who doesn't know how to raise kids**
- **The local church is the answer for the teenager, who has no idea why he is alive.**

- **The local church is where a person can go to learn how to better manage his finances.**
- **The local church is where a person can be trained to make his life useful and give it real meaning.**

You come up with an issue, of any magnitude, and the local church can help.

Now, the local church isn't the answer just because of what it is. It is the answer because of,
Who empowers it,
Jesus Christ

It is the answer because of,
Where it gets its message,
The Holy Word of God, and

It is the answer because of,
What it preaches,
The Gospel message of Salvation

You check it out, and you'll find out that there is no other organization, no other institution upon the face of this earth, ordained by God to accomplish what the local church does.

THE MISSION OF THE LOCAL CHURCH

God's mission for the local church is simple to understand but will take a lifetime to accomplish.

A. We are to win souls

I am convinced that the only reason you and I are not in heaven already tonight is because we are to win souls. Did you ever stop to think that everything the Christian is supposed to do, we can do better in heaven, except win souls?

- **We will be able to sing better in heaven**
- **We will be able to study our Bibles better in heaven**
- **We will be able to worship God better in heaven**

Church services will be better in heaven than they are here. Everything we do as Christians, we will be able to do better when we get to heaven.

Except for soul winning.

There is, therefore, nothing we could do on earth that is more important than soul winning. Unless you make an exception for training more soul winners. And the first part of that mission is to win souls and train those that it wins to win more souls.

But the mission does not end there.

B. We are to Baptize those Saved.

I get the impression that some folks think baptism is an optional command. Now, it is true that a person does not have to be baptized in order to be saved.

I think about when Jesus was baptized. I am confident that

Jesus would have gone to heaven even if He had not gotten baptized. He is the only begotten Son of God. He is co-equal and co-eternal with God the father. Jesus did not have to be baptized to go to heaven. But Jesus got baptized because he said, "*It becometh us to fulfill all righteousness.*" Jesus got baptized because it was the right thing to do. That is exactly the same reason why those who are already saved ought to get baptized.

- **It is the right thing to do**
- **It is the first step of obedience after you have gotten saved and**
- **It is a command of the Scriptures!**

It is a part of the mission God gave to the church.

There will be those who have excuses why they would not need to be baptized, or why they shouldn't or couldn't be baptized. Of course, you can't force a person into baptism, but the truth is, any Scriptural BAPTIST church will BAPTIZE as many as we can after they are saved.

But, the mission of the church does not end there either.

C. We are to teach them to observe all that Jesus Commanded.

This is the discipleship ministry of the church. Ours is not to win someone to Christ and then let them pick what type of church they want to go to. We do not have the privilege of witnessing to someone, winning them to Christ, and then to tell them, "*Now, be sure this Sunday to attend the congregation of your choice!*" If we believe what we preach and teach, then we are to bring as many of those we have won to Christ into the church as is possible for instruction in Christian living.

I am not too interested in home Bible study type groups. I don't think they are necessary. If a person will come to church Sunday morning, evening, and Wednesday, as well as Sunday school and the special services the church holds, they'll get all the discipleship they need.

Your mission is the GREAT COMMISSION.
Win souls,
Baptize the Saved, and
Teach them to obey the Lord.

THE METHODS OF THE LOCAL CHURCH

God has not given us the liberty to do whatever we please with HIS church.

We have no right to get the church off on any other mission than that given to us in the Bible. Nor do we have any right to use methods other than those prescribed within the pages of the Scripture. While I do think we can use some of the modern tools to help us accomplish our mission, the methods cannot change. At one time, a preacher would write out his message with a quill pen. Today, I type mine out on a computer. But the fact still remains, I preach.

God's methods for accomplishing the Great Commission are
A. Going
Matt 28:19
Mark 16:15
Acts 5:20

Our first method has to be TO GO. The Scriptures lay the burden for accomplishing the great commission upon us.
- **It is not the unsaved world's place to come to us so we can win them**
- **It is our place to talk to them so we can win them**

We cannot expect that, by hanging up a sign that says CHURCH, or placing an ad in the paper, people will naturally come to Christ. We must go to them. Where do we go?
- **We need to go to our friends and relatives, as Jesus**

commanded the demoniac of Gadara. then
- **We should go door to door and house to house, as Paul taught by his own example. finally**
- **We should go around the world through missions projects.**

I am of the firm conviction that no church is a scriptural church if it does not financially support missionaries outside their locale.

We accomplish our mission through the method of going.

We accomplish our missions secondly
B. Through the Method of Preaching
2 Timothy 4:2

- **Preaching is the proclamation of the good news of the Bible through a confident means.**
- **Preaching is considered foolish to the world and**
- **Preaching brings conviction.**

Preaching is declaring, "*Thus saith the Lord*."

Real preaching will always conclude with a decision to be made; with something the listener ought to do in order to get right or stay right with God.

God uses preaching,
- **To save the lost**
- **To recover the backslidden,**
- **To train the believer, and**
- **To rebuke the sinner**

The third method we have available in accomplishing the mission is
C. Through the fellowship of the believers.
God said way back in the Garden of Eden it is not good that man should be alone.

The most dangerous thing any Christian can do is to isolate themselves from other believers.
The church exists, among other things, as a means of fellowship and encouragement to keep on keeping on for Christ. You watch, and you will see that those Christian who prosper spiritually, are those who are faithful to church. They make the church the central point of their social life.

It is also dangerous for a church to think it can survive by itself.
In the Bible you will find churches cooperating together. Not controlling one another but working side by side for the cause of Christ.

Paul would write a letter to one church, then he would instruct them to let other churches read it too. Churches would band together to financially support Paul, or the poor Saints in Jerusalem.

Fellowship is a method God has given to help us accomplish our mission.

THE MANDATE OF THE LOCAL CHURCH
And that is, KEEP AT IT.

Jesus said, *"No man , having put his hand to the plough, and looking back, is fit for the kingdom of God."*

Paul said
"The gifts and calling of God are without repentance."

Another scripture says
"Take heed to the ministry ,which thou hast received in the Lord, that thou fulfil it."

A. Keep at it when you are discouraged
I have yet to know of a church that didn't go through rough

times. There will be trials of all sorts of variety.

- **People problems**
- **Money problems**

- **Attacks of the Devil and**
- **Attacks from the Lost.**

Just keep at it. Don't let discouragement cause you to quit your mission.

B. Keep at it when you are distracted

Probably, more dangerous than the rough times when Satan attacks, are the good times, when you are easily distracted from the mission.

More than one good church has been ruined when they were successful enough that they got their building paid for and full of people, so they quit winning souls and working at reaching more!

Don't let yourself get distracted from the mission. Don't let yourself get distracted with new methods, new Christian organizations, new ideas and plans.

- **You know what your mission is**
- **You know what the methods are**

Just keep at it.

Fundamentals Concerning Man

Chapter Twenty-Four
WHAT ABOUT ME?
Genesis 1:26-27

- **How am I here?**
- **What is my purpose?**
- **Where will I go when I die?**

These questions have been top among those asked for the recorded history of mankind. *Philosophy*, *Religion*, and even *Humanism* all exist for the most part to answer these questions.

And if you don't think they are important, **consider this**: as the average person becomes less and less interested in the answers to these questions, more and more frequently people are concluding that there is no good reason to continue living.

The statistics of suicide are staggering.
Actual Suicides[66]

- **1.3% of all deaths are from suicide.**
- **On average, one suicide occurs every 16 minutes.**
- **Suicide is the eleventh leading cause of death for all Americans.**
- **Suicide is the third leading cause of death for young people aged 15-24 year olds. (1st = accidents, 2nd = homicide)**
- **Suicide is the second leading cause of death for 25-34 year olds.**
- **Suicide is the second leading cause of death among college students.**
- **More males die from suicide than females. (4 male deaths by suicide for each female death by suicide.)**

---

[66] http://www.suicide.org/suicide-statistics.html#2005, accessed 10-15-13

- **More people die from suicide than from homicide. (Suicide ranks as the 11th leading cause of death; Homicide ranks 13th.)**
- **There were over 800,000 suicide attempts in 2005**

- **Twice as many people ages 15-24 committed suicide in 2005 as did in 1950**
- **Three times as many ages 15-19**
- **Twice as many ages 20-24**
- **A third more ages 25-34**

What this suggests is that, the further we get from 1963 and the banning of the Bible and prayer in public schools, the more inclined a person might be to opt to cut off his own life rather than address the challenges of life.

It is impossible not to see that life on planet earth can be
- **Brutal**
- **Difficult and**
- **Downright depressing**

By the way - it makes no difference whether you are
- **Wealthy**
- **Educated or**
- **Influential**

Life can get the best of you.

Isn't it Dan Rather, the well known and very successful news journalist, who has advocated for those with depression by admitting that he has fought with severe depression?

Thoughtful souls have chosen to wrestle with these troubles rather than to give in to them. And it is not surprising that God would want to give us the tools both to wrestle with those questions that give meaning to life and the very answers to them.

So, once the Bible has declared to us that God is - it goes right into that basic question man has always sought to answer:

- **How did I come to be?**
- **How did I get here?**
- **How is it that I exist, and that I exist in such a different state than the animals?**

And we learn right away that, in the beginning, God created not only the heavens and the earth, but you and me.

I want to give three fundamental questions the Word of God answers about our existence:

WE ARE CREATED

Genesis 1:27 KJV

So God created man ...

I know that evolutionary science claims that this did not happen. They want you to believe, in fact they teach your children that we are in fact, not the product of creation but of series of accidental events that run complete contrary to all observable truth.

- **Sometime**
- **Somewhere**
- **Somehow**

- **Nobody knows when**
- **Nobody knows why**
- **Nobody knows how**

A series of inanimate elements came together and became animated - they sprang to life. And then over the course of billions of years that living glob

- **Sometime**
- **Somewhere**
- **Somehow**

- **Nobody knows when**
- **Nobody knows why**
- **Nobody knows how**

began to mutate and change.

But instead of mutating in a negative manner, like everything we have ever been able to witness does, this glob of life mutated positively.

And not only that but,
- **Sometime**
- **Somewhere**
- **Somehow**

- **Nobody knows when**
- **Nobody knows why**
- **Nobody knows how**

It mutated positively over and over and over again over the course of billions and billions of years.

- **Sometime**
- **Somewhere**
- **Somehow**

- **Nobody knows when**
- **Nobody knows why**
- **Nobody knows how**

This glob of life ran opposite the stream of observable science and continued to mutate into better and better globs of life until finally, that glob could write.
- **Sometime**
- **Somewhere**
- **Somehow**

- **Nobody knows when**
- **Nobody knows why**
- **Nobody knows how**

I know that is what evolutionary science teaches is how man came into existence. But God gives a much more elegant and reasonable answer - one that requires much less imagination and faith.

God simply says He created us.

We are not the products of accidental mutation. We are not the result of some cruel twist of fate that kept making us better and better and better until we could finally look around us and see that everything is getting worse and worse.

God,
- **Purposely**
- **Intelligently and**
- **Meticulously**

created our early parents and gave to them the power to reproduce themselves. God considered what He had already created and then said within Himself
Genesis 1:26 KJV
... Let us make man .....

That very fact that I am not an accident, if internalized and made a part of my character, changes
- **The way I see my life and**
- **The attitude I have toward living it**

WE ARE CREATED IN THE IMAGE OF GOD
Genesis 1:26-27 KJV
And God said, Let us make man in our image, after our likeness: and let them have dominion over the fish of the sea, and over the fowl of the air, and over the cattle, and over all the earth, and over every creeping thing that creepeth upon the earth.
So God created man in his own image, in the image of God created he him; male and female created he them.

Now I learn that,
- **I am not only created on purpose, but**
- **I am created with design**

I want you to notice three things concerning our creation in the image of God:
A. Expresses love of God

It is easy to see the difference between God's creation of the heavens and the earth and His creation of mankind.

God spoke into existence
- **The skies**
- **The oceans**
- **The earth**
- **The moon**
- **The stars**

He spake into existence
- **The air**
- **The grass**
- **The light and**
- **The trees**

God spake into existence
- **The birds of the air**
- **The fish of the seas**
- **The beasts of the field and**
- **The critters of the earth**

But then it is as if God paused in His creative process. He stopped talking to nothing and making something ... and He spoke to himself.

And God said, Let us make man <u>in our image</u>

This is a new thing. This is different than all of the rest of His creation.

The account is given more detail in,
Genesis 2:7 KJV
And the LORD God formed man of the dust of the ground, and breathed into his nostrils the breath of life; and man became a living soul.
- **He didn't just speak him into existence**
- **He didn't make him and let him be**

God formed the man out of the dust of the ground. The language indicates that God literally scooped up some ground and molded the man from it. But even more than that, He breathed into the man his very life.

We are created beings - that's for sure. But we bear in our bodies the very breath of God.

That's love.

Within the church I pastor are a ton of little children. I cherish all of them.

- **I love their stories of fishing**
- **I love to hear them tell me about their favorite toys or activities**
- **I treasure getting to share with them just a few minutes of fun and games**

But in this church, there are also three very special little children. To everyone else in the church they are just like the rest of the kids that are,

- **Six or**
- **Five or**
- **One**

But I see something very different in those three. I see my own life and breath.

They exist because I have existed. They exist because in September of 1979 I met a young lady named Anita and in September of 1980 she became my bride.

And these three little children; ages

- **Six and**
- **Five and**
- **One**

carry our image and likeness.

Knowing that God created me in His image and that He loves me, when made a part of my character and being, gives vigor and energy to my daily life.

That I am created in the image of God

B. Answers why I am different than the animals

We are different than the animals because we were created differently than the animals. There is no missing link in the evolutionary process between the animals and mankind because there is no link.

- **Man was created the same day as the animals but**
- **Man was not created in the same way as the animals**

Whatever biological similarities that exist between man and animals is simply attributed to having the same creator; which, by the way, makes much more sense than the idea that

- **a series of random mutations taking place over**
- **a series of billions of years**

could produce

- **So many unique creatures with**
- **So many similar features**

and then, that I am created in the image of God

C. Implies an eternal existence rather than a temporal one

Genesis 2:17 KJV

But of the tree of the knowledge of good and evil, thou shalt not eat of it: for in the day that thou eatest thereof thou shalt surely die.

God warned them that if they arte of this particular fruit they would sure die, which indicates that if they had not eaten that fruit they would not have died.

I think it is fascinating that the medical science has two problems with life:

- **Number one - they don't know what makes alive**
- **Number two, they don't know what makes it die**

God created our bodies to live forever.

And, according to the Bible, they do live forever somewhere - either heaven or hell.

The good news of the Bible is that, God gets us through how sin broke what God created in a hurry (by the end of Genesis chapter three) and spends the rest of the Bible describing how He plans to fix what has been broken through the promise of Jesus Christ.

WE ARE CREATED TO FELLOWSHIP
Genesis 2:18 KJV
And the LORD God said, It is not good that the man should be alone; I will make him an help meet for him.

I know that when we first read these words what immediately comes to mind is marriage; *a man needs a wife*. But I want to suggest to you that marriage is only one element of what we will find out in the Bible is a multifaceted truth.

It is not good for man to be alone:
A. A man needs a relationship with his wife
So God early created for Adam a helpmeet
B. A man needs a relationship with his family
We find Adam and Eve having children
C. A man needs a relationship with a community
God instituted human government just after the Flood
D. A man needs a membership in a church
Which is the New Testament answer to a truth that is presented throughout the Bible - people need to provoke one another to love and worship God
E. A man needs a relationship with God
I believe this to be the ultimate message in Genesis 2:18.

I do not believe it would be wrong to say what goes for Adam also goes for Eve.

The woman needs a husband every bit as much as the man needs a wife - and so it goes with all the other relationships:

- **A spouse provides** *completion*
- **A family provides future** *generations*
- **A community provides** *protection*
- **A church provides** *exhortation*
- **God provides** *redemption* **and** *salvation*

Remember what Jesus said were the two great commandments:
Matthew 22:37-39 KJV
Jesus said unto him, Thou shalt love the Lord thy God with all thy heart, and with all thy soul, and with all thy mind.
This is the first and great commandment.
And the second is like unto it, Thou shalt love thy neighbour as thyself.

What we find in the Bible is a weaving of these two types of relationships.

- **We can't really love people unless we love God and**
- **If we don't love people, we do not love God**

The most important thing I can ever do in my life is love the Lord. And I need to love others in order to love God.

Every thinking person in human history has wrestled with the question of our being. Every person that is, except those

- **Like Moses**
- **Like David and**
- **Like Daniel**

These were men who knew what it was like to suffer but also knew that their life was created on purpose - so they lived their lives to the fullest. So we have a choice,

- **Will we continue to wrestle and struggle with all of the why questions of life?**
- **Or will be accept that God created us and that He created us with a purpose?**
- **Will we trust Him to save us and forgive us of our sin nature?** and being saved
- **Will we trust Him to direct us into a life - not of ease - but of abundance?**

Chapter Twenty-Five

SIN'S EFFECT ON OUR RELATIONSHIP WITH GOD

Genesis 3:1-11

The book of Genesis is foundational to everything else that is taught in the Bible. In it we find the beginning of everything we know except God, who has had no beginning. In Genesis three we have the account of the original sin. And since the Bible assures us that there is nothing new under the sun, there are no new surprises about sin either.

Sin has always been exactly what sin was when Adam and Eve first sinned.

SIN IS REBELLION AGAINST GOD

Vs 1-7

I see rebellion all through these verses.
- **There is the rebellion of the serpent (Satan)**
- **There is rebellion in the tone of the voice of the Devil (Ye shall not surely die)**
- **There is rebellion in the tenor of Eve's voice (ye shall not eat ye neither shall ye touch it lest ye die.)**

Sin is always against God.
- **While our sin might affect others**
- **While our sin may be pointed at somebody else**

Sin is always first and foremost sin against God.

Satan's attack on Eve was an attack on God. And Eve, whether she wanted that way or not, attacked God when she disobeyed God.

It is rebellion to,
A. Listen to one who rebel against God.

Vs 1

Frankly, Eve had no business even listening to the serpent tempt her to sin. If she had been doing right, she would have run as soon as she heard that the serpent's conversation was going to be anti-God.

Christian, you really have no business allowing a person to lead you in a conversation that is anti God. As soon as a person approaches a subject that is dishonoring
- **To God**
- **To His Bible or**
- **To His church**

You ought to just stomp your foot and put a prompt end to the conversation.
- **I am not talking about those conversations when a person is listening to you tell them truth and they do not believe it**
- **I am talking about those conversations where they are controlling the conversation and it is opposed to what you know to be truth**

Put a sudden end to the conversation and get out of there. It is rebellion against God to do otherwise.

2 John 1:9
Whosoever transgresseth, and abideth not in the doctrine of Christ, hath not God. He that abideth in the doctrine of Christ, he hath both the Father and the Son. (KJV)

It is rebellion to,
B. Want to be your own God
Vs 5

That is the sin that led Lucifer to fall heaven and to take the roll of Satan. He said, "I will be like the most high God" Once you take the position that you want to control things yourself. Once you determine to,
- **Run your own life and**

- **Make your own decisions and**
- **Do your own thing**

You have just taken control from God. You have said, "*I will be like the most high…*" It is rebellion!
- **It is rebellion to think you are above the rules**
- **It is rebellion to think you know better than the Bible**
- **It is rebellion to think you can do as you please**

It is rebellion to listen to those who rebel against God
It is rebellion to want to be your own God and

It is rebellion to,
C. Lead others in your sin
Satan led Eve to sin as he had sinned and Eve led Adam to sin as she had sinned.

You can be assured of this, if you run with sinners, they will try for all they are worth to get you to sin with them! That is one of the reasons that Christians are to separate themselves from those who walk not according to the things we are taught in the Bible.

You become who you want to be by being with people who are what you want to be. You cannot possibly become what God wants you to be by hanging around people who are not what God wants them to be. That is why we Christians are always harping about making the right kinds of friends. There is something rebellious about hanging around those who live in sin. And it is rebellious to try to get people to sin with you.

SIN RUINS OUR FELLOWSHIP WITH GOD
Vs 8-10

God created Adam and Eve to fellowship with Him.
- **He created us so we could talk with Him**

- **So we could love Him and be loved by Him**
- **He created us so we could walk with Him**

Adam and Eve's sin destroyed that.

After they sinned, we find them
A. Hiding from God instead of hurrying to God.
Vs 8

I imagine things were different before their sin. I imagine that before they sinned, they looked forward to hearing the voice of God and walking with Him in the cool of the day.
- **Before they sinned, they watched for God to come down from heaven**
- **Before they sinned, they hurried to His side when He arrived**
- **Before they sinned, they were excited and happy to be with God**

But after they sinned, they hid from Him.

A lot of people are hiding from God today.
- **They won't come to church**
- **They won't listen to a preacher**
- **They won't read the Bible**
- **They won't pray**

It is because they know they are not right with God.

I saw where Adam and Eve hid among the trees. That is ironic. They are using the wonderful things God gave them to hide from the God who gave it to them. Just like those who run to the mountains:
- **Or to the ocean**
- **Or to the fishing lake**
- **Or to the job**
- **Or to the parents**
- **Or to the kids**

They use the things God gave them as an excuse to hide from the very God who gave it to them!

After they sinned, they were

B. Afraid of God instead of awed by God
Vs 10

Instead of having that sense of wonder and love and awe for God, after they sinned, they were afraid.

That is a right response by the way. Because God is holy and just, He was not going to let them get away with their sin. The fear of the Lord is the beginning of wisdom. The smartest thing any of us can do is fear the judgment of God.

But there is no fellowship around fear. Fellowship comes when; after we have been chastised, we do right by God. Sin makes it where you simply cannot be close to God
- **You can't enjoy life**
- **You can't enjoy your loved ones**
- **You can't enjoy your job**

When you don't enjoy fellowship with God you won't enjoy anything.

SIN WRECKS OUR RELATIONSHIP TO GOD
Vs 11-24

Before Adam and Eve sinned, they were children of God. After they sinned, they were children of the devil. Because of their sin we are all born onto this planet as children of the devil. We have to be born again to be born into the family of God and become sons of God. Sin wrecks our relationship to God.

A. Their conversation with God was accusatory instead of kind
Vs 11-16

I conduct conversations with my children differently than I do with strangers. The conversation we find in these verses is certainly not the kind that you would expect from a father to his children.

- **There are fingers pointed**
- **There is judgment meted**
- **There are accusations flying**

I know that when the Christian sins He cannot lose his relationship as a child of God. But sin does wreck the wonder of that relationship.

B. The earth was cursed instead of cooperative
Vs 17-19

Before they had sinned, the earth brought forth abundantly for them. Before they sinned, work was a blessing: labor was out of love. Now all of a sudden work became drudgery and difficult.

And those who are the most involved in sin feel that way the most about their work. I would hate to have to get up and hate going to work every day. But the child of God, who knows that he is right with God, can do any work with joy in his heart because he knows he is doing it as unto the Lord.

C. The garden became prohibited instead of provided.
Vs 22-24

Before Adam and Eve sinned, they lived in a virtual paradise. After their sin God drove them from the garden and placed Cherubim with flaming swords to keep them from ever going in again.
- **What was once provided as a standard**
- **Was now prohibited with the sword.**

I think the Garden of Eden looks like heaven. Because of sin there are angels blocking the doors to heaven. Sin has separated between us and God so that we cannot come to Him.

- **Inside is eternal life**
- **Inside is joy and peace**
- **Inside is rest**

Inside is a renewed relationship with God almighty. We just can't get there.

- **The doors are blocked**
- **The gates are shut.**
- **The walls are too high for us to ever climb.**

But then there is Jesus. He said in John 10:9

I am the door: by me if any man enter in, he shall be saved, and shall go in and out, and find pasture. (KJV)

Sin has ruined everything. But Jesus came to save us from our sins. God made Him to be sin for us, who knew no sin, that we might be made the righteousness of God in Him.

Chapter Twenty-Six
THE GOSPEL IN A VERSE
1 Timothy 1:15

When we get right down to it, the Bible has one fundamental, basic purpose - to spread the news that:
"Christ Jesus came into the world to save sinners…"

- **Before God created the heavens and the earth**
- **Before Adam and Eve had taken their first breaths and**
- **Before Satan had ever conceived his plan to tempt them to sin**

God had already determined that, *"Christ Jesus [would come] into the world to save sinners…"*

Here is the whole Gospel in a nutshell. This verse explains in the briefest of words the full story of the life of Christ.
- **Why did Christ come into this world?**
- **Why did Christ allow Himself to be killed?**
- **Why did Christ rise from the grave in victory?**

TO SAVE SINNERS

I want to take a closer look at this fundamental verse and examine
- **Our nature**
- **Our need**
- **His Name**

OUR NATURE
Christ Jesus came into the world to save SINNERS

The whole work of Christ on this earth ***was for sinners***. So much so that the person who denies his sinfulness denies his need for Christ. He denies the work of God on his behalf.

Jesus said, John 9:39-41

And Jesus said, For judgment I am come into this world, that they which see not might see; and that they which see might be made blind. And some of the Pharisees which were with him heard these words, and said unto him, Are we blind also?
Jesus said unto them, If ye were blind, ye should have no sin: but now ye say, We see; therefore your sin remaineth. (KJV)

Get hold of what He has said. Only those who accept the fact that they are sinners receive forgiveness. Jesus said, "*I am come to seek and to save that which was lost.*"[67] If you refuse to admit that you are lost you also refuse the salvation of the Lord. We are by nature sinful. But Christ Jesus came into the world to save sinners.

Jesus came to save:
A. All sorts of sinners
As long as you fall into the general description of sinner, Christ came to save you. It doesn't matter what kind of sinner you are:
- **Gross sin or**
- **Great sin**

Christ came to save you.
- **Petty sin or**
- **Paltry sin**

Christ came to save you
- **Childish sin or**
- **Chastizable sin**

Christ came to save you

- **Everyone has sinned.**
  - But not everyone has sinned in the same way.
- **All men have wandered astray.**
  - But all have taken separate paths of sin

But no matter.
Christ came to save
- **Respectable sinners as well as**

---

[67] Luke 19:10

- **Despicable sinners**

Christ is willing to save
- **Proud sinners as well as**
- **Despairing sinners**

Christ came to save
- **The high classed social drinker as well as**
- **The drunk bum on the street.**

Christ came to save
- **The sinful family man as well as**
- **The homosexual**

No matter what kind of sinner a person is there is hope. Christ came into the world to save sinners. If there is a person who is not a sinner, Christ did not come for that one. They have nothing to do with Christ. But all sinners, of any sort can find hope in the work of Christ.

Christ came to save,
B. Any sinner

The sinner does not have to be
- **Humble or**
- **Repentant or**
- **Softened**
in order to ask for and expect salvation.

Because Christ will
- **Soften the heart**
- **Give humility and**
- **Cause repentance**

Christ came to save sinners,
C. While they are still in their sin
Romans 5:8

But God commendeth his love toward us, in that, while we were yet sinners, Christ died for us. (KJV)

A sinner does not have to clean up in order to be saved. Rather, Christ Himself will clean up the one whom He has saved.

In His earthly life Christ always met sinners where they were. He associated with publicans and sinners for those were the ones He came to save.

You don't need to wait until you are better to visit the Great Physician. Bring your sinful disease to Him and He will heal.

The only requirement in order to be saved is to be a sinner. And we are all are - SINNERS. All have sinned and come short of the glory of God. There is none righteous no not one.

Isaiah 53:6
All we like sheep have gone astray; we have turned every one to his own way; and the LORD hath laid on him the iniquity of us all. (KJV)

Romans 3:11-12
There is none that understandeth, there is none that seeketh after God. They are all gone out of the way, they are together become unprofitable; there is none that doeth good, no, not one. (KJV)

By nature, we are all sinners. Have you sincerely admitted your sinfulness to God?

OUR NEED
Christ came into the world to SAVE sinners.

We are in need of salvation. And Christ came to give it.

The reason Jesus:

- **Came and**
- **Died and**
- **Rose again**

is because without the salvation of Christ sinful men are destined to eternal torments in hell. If this were not true, then Christ died for naught.

Sinners need to be saved. It is an unfortunate truth from the Bible though that not all sinners get saved. John 1:11
He came unto his own, and his own received him not. (KJV)

I John 5:12
He that hath the Son hath life; and he that hath not the Son of God hath not life. (KJV)

Salvation is available to all sinners, but it is not received by all sinners.

What does it mean to be saved?

We are saved from,
A. The punishment of sin
That punishment is death
For the wages of sin is death[68]

Death passed upon all men for that all have sinned[69].

The ultimate death is eternal separation from God in the Lake of Fire.
Revelation 21:8
But the fearful, and unbelieving, and the abominable, and murderers, and whoremongers, and sorcerers, and idolaters, and all liars, shall have their part in the lake which burneth with fire and brimstone: which is the second death. (KJV)

---

[68] Romans 6:23
[69] Romans 5:12

Salvation by Christ is salvation from the punishment of sin which is the second death.

That when we get saved, we escape eternal hell is grand enough. But we are also saved from,

B. The position of sin

Christ forgives of the sins we have already committed, washes them away in His own blood. And the Father even forgets that we ever committed those sins. Then He blesses us with the freedom from the guilty conscience of those sins.

We are saved from

C. The propensity to sin

So that we no longer *must* sin. He frees us from the bondage to sin that all of us have experienced so that we may still sin occasionally, but it not longer controls us as it once did.

What is more, this **salvation is permanent**. Christ saves our souls through no work of our own and He keeps us saved through no work of our own.

Philippians 1:6

Being confident of this very thing, that he which hath begun a good work in you will perform it until the day of Jesus Christ: (KJV)

Our need is salvation from our sin. And Christ came into this world for that very reason. Salvation therefore is the reasonable choice for all to make.

HIS NAME
CHRIST JESUS came into this world to save sinners

Salvation for sinful man is not:
- **In the best of men nor**
- **In an angel from heaven but**
- **In Christ Jesus**

The word Christ means, **"anointed**." Christ Jesus was anointed by God to be the Saviour of the World. Christ is a perfect Saviour, especially fitted and qualified for the work that He has done. So that, *"there is none other name under heaven given among men whereby we must be saved."*[70] Christ Jesus is the only anointed Saviour that there is.

John 3:16
For God so love the world that He gave His only begotten son that whosoever believeth in Him should not perish but have everlasting life.

There is only one Saviour.

So many faiths believe that Christ is one of many ways to be saved. Some even profess to be Christians who say, "As long as you believe in God it does not matter what you believe His name is."

That is simply not the testimony of the infallible Word of God. Salvation for sinners comes only by faith in His name.

The question then is, "Are you certain that Christ Jesus has saved you?"

---

[70] Acts 4:12

Chapter Twenty-Seven
WHAT IS THE RAPTURE?
1 Thessalonians 4:13-18

It is time to shift to the last set of fundamental doctrines, those having to do with "last things." The idea of what will happen in the future

- **Is a joke to the unbelieving world**
- **Is a matter of question and debate among many in the religious world**
- **Is often avoided by many in the Christian world**

But I would like to remind you that *the peace of God for today rests almost completely on trusting Him for what happens in our future.* So, understanding the prophetic things really is fundamental.

Let me begin with a brief overview of the entire theme of the Lord's Return:

A. Shortly after Adam and Eve sinned God promised them that one would come from the seed of a woman and bruise the head of the serpent.[71] This was the first promise that someone would come to deliver man from his sin.

B. Later on God promised Abraham that from the children of Abraham, specifically the Jews, would come on in whom all the nations of the world would be blessed.

---

[71] Genesis 3:15 KJV
And I will put enmity between thee and the woman, and between thy seed and her seed; it shall bruise thy head, and thou shalt bruise his heel.

C. And much later on Isaiah prophesied
Isaiah 9:6

"For unto us a child is born, unto us a Son is given, and the government shall be upon His shoulder: and His name shall be called Wonderful, Counselor, the Mighty God, the Everlasting Father, the Prince of Peace."

D. All through history the godly Jews were waiting for the Lord to come and deliver them from their sin. And the godly Jews expected Him to be born of a woman. This is the idea of the Lord's first appearance as a man to men on earth.

It was also promised that this One who would take away sin would be Israel's king forever and ever. In 2 Samuel 7:16 the Bible says,

And thine house and thy kingdom shall be established for ever before thee: thy throne shall be established for ever. (KJV)

And in Psalm 45:6 I read,

Thy throne, O God, is for ever and ever: the sceptre of thy kingdom is a right sceptre. (KJV)

- When Jesus came the first time He came as a child born in a manger in Bethlehem and He died to pay for the sins of the world.
- When Jesus comes to earth again, He will come in great power to establish His kingdom for ever and ever!

According to Revelation 19, when He comes to do that, He will bring His saints with Him.[72]

Somewhere between that *first coming* and the *future second*

---

[72] Revelation 19:11-14 KJV

And I saw heaven opened, and behold a white horse; and he that sat upon him was called Faithful and True, and in righteousness he doth judge and make war.

His eyes were as a flame of fire, and on his head were many crowns; and he had a name written, that no man knew, but he himself.

And he was clothed with a vesture dipped in blood: and his name is called The Word of God.

And the armies which were in heaven followed him upon white horses, clothed in fine linen, white and clean.

coming, all of the Christians will have to be taken to heaven so that they can return with Jesus. That point, when the Christians are taken up to heaven, we call the Rapture.

We have no real idea when the rapture will take place.
- **The Bible gives no signs so that we can get ready. and**
- **There is nothing stopping it from taking place at this very moment, except the secret will of God**

We don't know when it will happen, but we can tell a lot about what it will be like when it happens.

In 1 Thessalonians 4:17 you won't find the word rapture. Instead you see the words, "**caught up**." referring to the rapture. "Caught up" is translated from the Greek word "rapto." That word has several meanings, all of which describe the rapture.

TO CATCH AWAY SPEEDILY

When the rapture does take place and all the Christians are taken to heaven, it is going to happen FAST.

1 Corinthians 15:51-52
Behold, I shew you a mystery; We shall not all sleep, but we shall all be changed,
In a moment, in the twinkling of an eye, at the last trump: for the trumpet shall sound, and the dead shall be raised incorruptible, and we shall be changed. (KJV)

I have heard that the twinkling of an eye is in the "mille-seconds." That is quicker that the eye can see. What this means is that it is going to be sudden and unexpected. It will come like a thief in the night, the Bible says. And you will not have time to prepare unless you prepare ahead of time and stay that way. Unsaved people won't even know it happened until it is over.

Imagine the chaos caused by cars going down the highway and all of a sudden, the driver is gone. Or the pilot of the airliner is gone. Those kinds of things are speculation but very possible.

I don't know how the unsaved that are left on this earth will explain how so many people disappeared at one time, but I am sure that it will create sudden chaos and confusion.

The rapture will happen quickly. If you aren't saved, you need to get saved now so that you are ready when it does happen.

TO SEIZE BY FORCE

As tragic as it is, there are some Christians who love this world and the things they have acquired in it. They won't want to go to heaven when the Lord calls them. Christians should never allow themselves to get so caught up in the affairs of this life that they are anxious to get caught up into heaven.

I wonder sometimes if God doesn't allow us to suffer so often so that we keep our eyes off of this world and keep them looking forward to heaven.

Illustration:
The story of Lot in Genesis 19:
The Bible teaches that Lot was a just and righteous ma but he moved to the wicked city of Sodom and grew to like it there. We don't know how long he lived in Sodom, but eventually the city got so wicked that God chose to destroy it. But He couldn't do it with Lot there. God sent two angels to warn Lot and tell Him to take his family and leave town. But Lot was so involved in the affairs of Sodom that the angels eventually had to take him by the hand and drag him out of the city.

That is a tragic story. But I know some Christians that, if the

Lord came today, He would have to drag them to heaven.

TO CLAIM FOR ONE'S SELF

If you are a real Christian, you need to come to grips with the Bible fact that you are not your own. You have been bought with a price.[73] And that price is the blood of Jesus.[74] If you are a Christian Jesus owns you. He paid for you with His own life. And you are obligated to glorify God

- **In your body and**
- **In your spirit**

That is not bad because the other choice is to belong to the devil and to live your life glorifying him. And that is what all the unsaved people do. When Jesus calls for the rapture, He is going to take all those that He has bought to be with Him.

Ephesians 5:27 says He will,
"present it to Himself a glorious church not having spot or wrinkle or any such thing!"

This also lets us know that only those that are His are going. 1 Thessalonians 4:13-18 says that only those that are "in Christ" will go. You can almost always tell who is in Christ because,
2 Corinthians 5:17 says
If any man be in Christ he is a new creature, old things are passed away, behold all things are become new.

---

[73] 1 Corinthians 6:19-20 KJV
What? know ye not that your body is the temple of the Holy Ghost which is in you, which ye have of God, and ye are not your own?
For ye are bought with a price: therefore glorify God in your body, and in your spirit, which are God's.
[74] Acts 20:28 KJV
Take heed therefore unto yourselves, and to all the flock, over the which the Holy Ghost hath made you overseers, to feed the church of God, which he hath purchased with his own blood.

Real Christians act differently than the rest of the world.

TO MOVE TO A NEW PLACE
Jesus said,
John 14:2-3
In my Father's house are many mansions: if it were not so, I would have told you. I go to prepare a place for you.
And if I go and prepare a place for you, I will come again, and receive you unto myself; that where I am, there ye may be also. (KJV)

We Christians have a dual citizenship:
- **We are citizens of this earth and**
- **We are citizens of heaven.**

And actually, we are supposed to serve as spokesmen for our heavenly home. But when the rapture happens, then our job on this earth will be done. At that time, it will be "Home - here we come." We will be pulling up stakes down here and settling in with Jesus Christ our Lord.

TO RESCUE FROM DANGER
That tells us something very important about the rapture; tt will take place **before** the terrible Tribulation that will try this world.

I know some disagree with this, but **there is no way to put all of the rapture verses together** and fairly and literally interpret them without believing in what we call the Pre-tribulational rapture. It doesn't take much sense to see that this world is getting pretty rough. Just in the last few years alone we have witnessed
- **Many states approving same sex marriages**
- **Many others refusing to oppose them**
- **Forced health care**
- **Falling economy**
- **Muslims in placed in the highest offices of our land**

and the Bible teaches that it is going to get worse. It will get worse than the world has ever known. When this Tribulation starts, there will not be a Christian one on the earth. Look at

1 Thessalonians 1:10
And to wait for his Son from heaven, whom he raised from the dead, even Jesus, which delivered us from the wrath to come. (KJV)

Christians have been delivered already from the wrath to come.

Another verse is Colossians 1:13
Who hath delivered us from the power of darkness and hath translated us into the kingdom of His dear Son.

And there is Revelation 3:10
Because thou hast kept the word of my patience, I also will keep thee from the hour of temptation, which shall come upon all the world, to try them that dwell upon the earth. (KJV)

Christians don't need to be tried; Jesus was already tried for us. He literally took the wrath of God for us so that we wouldn't have to. As a matter of fact, God, I believe, is actually withholding His wrath until the Christians are all gone. That's what He did with Lot, remember? I believe that is what is being referred to in 2 Thessalonians 2:3-8 and especially verses 6-7.

2 Thessalonians 2:3-8
Let no man deceive you by any means: for that day shall not come, except there come a falling away first, and that man of sin be revealed, the son of perdition;
Who opposeth and exalteth himself above all that is called God, or that is worshipped; so that he as God sitteth in the temple of God, shewing himself that he is God.
Remember ye not, that, when I was yet with you, I told you these things?
And now ye know what withholdeth that he might be revealed in his time.
For the mystery of iniquity doth already work: only he who now letteth will let, until he be taken out of the way.
And then shall that Wicked be revealed, whom the Lord shall consume with the spirit of his mouth, and shall destroy with the brightness of his coming: (KJV)

Just to summarize this doctrine of the rapture:

1. There is nothing that could stop it from happening today.

No man knows the day or the hour, so the Bible tells us to always be ready and you prepare for the rapture by getting saved.

2. The Rapture will be complete.

All Christians will hear the trumpet. Every Christian will be taken.

3. Your only chance to be saved is before the rapture.

The Bible does teach that multitudes of souls will be saved during the Tribulation, but the Bible also teaches that those who rejected the chance to get saved before the rapture will believe a lie after the rapture and not get saved.

For all of us that are saved and living right with God, all of this is exciting. If it is not exciting to you

- **Maybe you need to get saved**
- **Maybe you need to get right with God**

Chapter Twenty-Eight
HE'S COMING BACK
Revelation 19:11-21

When it comes to prophecy, there are some details we can't know for sure. But there is a basic outline of future events that is certain, sure and, I believe, fundamentals.

1. The next event to take place is the Rapture of the Christians
It will include the resurrection of those Christians who have died when Jesus comes.

2. That is followed by a seven-year Tribulation that will come to try the people left on the earth.
It is divided into two halves
The first half, I think, is marked by worldwide tragedy. Cataclysms like we have not yet seen. Things that will make:
- **The Tsunami of 2004**
- **Hurricane Katrina (New Orleans)**
- **Hurricane Sandy (New York) and now**
- **Typhoon Yolanda (the Philippines) 2013**

look like spring drizzles.

The second half is marked by the unbridled terror of Antichrist against all of humanity – especially those who will not worship him. Jesus said of the Tribulation:
Matthew 24:22 KJV
And except those days should be shortened, there should no flesh be saved...

3. At the end of those seven years,
- **Jesus will return to this earth.**
- **He will defeat Antichrist and those who have followed him and**
- **He will establish a kingdom on the earth lasting 1000 years**

When those 1000 years are completed, Satan will have one final battle against the Lord. He will lose.

4. God will then judge those who have never gotten saved in what the Bible calls "The Great White Throne Judgment".

5. At the end of that judgment God will give to those who have been faithful a
- **New Heaven**
- **New Earth and**
- **New Jerusalem**

where we will live forever in His presence. I have left out some important details, but this is a general schematic of what's left in prophecy.

I want to take you to the end of that seven-year Tribulation.
Imagine now that you have just endured those seven terrible years. No doubt you have witnessed the traumatic deaths of many of your friends and loved ones as those years progressed through
- **Some of them likely died of starvation**
- **Some of them were the victims of supernatural disasters**
- **You may know some who died as enemies of the state – they refused to take the sign of the Beast and were executed for it**

You yourself, though not a believer seven years previous to this, have come to accept that Jesus Christ is indeed the Lord and Saviour and because of your faith, you have suffered great trials of persecution. But you have – somehow-survived. The sky has been unusual for some time and the rumors running round is that it is a sign from heaven. Jesus is coming back.

Antichrist has assembled the largest army he is able to in the valley of Megiddo, some miles north east of Jerusalem. And in a moment, the world as you know it is changed.

- Antichrist and his false prophet are defeated and cast into the bottomless pit.
- Kings and princes, complicit with the Antichrist, have died in the battle
- The armies of men and women who have enforced the reign of terror have been exterminated
- Jesus has come to set up His one-thousand-year kingdom.

If the Bible is true at all
- Jesus will come again
- Jesus will come again personally and
- Jesus will as a King

I want to describe for you what happens when Jesus comes again to begin His **One Thousand Year Reign**.

THE JEWS PROMISES ARE FULFILLED
Genesis 49:10 KJV
The sceptre shall not depart from Judah, nor a lawgiver from between his feet, until Shiloh come; and unto him shall the gathering of the people be.

We sometimes confuse the promises for Israel with the promises that God made to Christians, but they are very different.
- Israel's promises all have to do with their nation
- Christian promises all have to do with a congregation

- Israel's promises all have to do with God
- Christian promises all have to do with Christ

- Israel's promises all have to do with an earthly kingdom
- Christian promises all have to do eternal heaven

The world has been devastated in the past by Christian denominations who believed that Christian promises were earthly "kingdom" type promises.

- It's why the Catholics ruled kings

- **It's why the Protestants fragmented and persecuted anyone who did not believe just like they did**

Christian promises all have to do with heaven. **But it was always the promise to the Jews that they would become a great nation**. It was also always their promise that one from the tribe of Judah and specifically the family of David would rule on the throne of David in that Kingdom.

When Jesus comes to the earth again, He will fulfill all those promises to the Jews. (I believe the promises to the Christians will have all been fulfilled at the time of the rapture.)

There is some room for disagreement right here, but it is because of these differences of promises that **I do not see the Jews who have died in the faith being resurrected at the same time as the New Testament Saints.** I believe they are resurrected at the beginning of this one-thousand-year Kingdom. I also believe they are resurrected, not with glorified bodies as the Christians are, but with perfect and immortal bodies, similar to what Adam and Eve would have had before they fell in sin.

This millennial kingdom will be the culmination of every:
- **Promise God made to Abraham, Isaac and Jacob.**
- **Promises to David and to Solomon**
- **Promises to Jeremiah and to Daniel**

Promises that God refused to change His mind about even when Israel dove into her deepest days of idolatry and sin.

2 Kings 8:18-19 KJV
And he walked in the way of the kings of Israel, as did the house of Ahab: for the daughter of Ahab was his wife: and he did evil in the sight of the LORD.
Yet the LORD would not destroy Judah for David his servant's sake, as he promised him to give him alway a light, and to his children.

During the one thousand year reign,
THE LORD RULES WITH A ROD OF IRON
Revelation 19:15 KJV
And out of his mouth goeth a sharp sword, that with it he should smite the nations: and he shall rule them with a rod of iron: and he treadeth the winepress of the fierceness and wrath of Almighty God.

Seems to me that we Christians get a lot of things having to do with future events mixed up.

We think of the,
- **Old Testament times as being when God was strict but**
- **New Testament times God is lenient.**

We think
- **The age of God as a taskmaster during the age of the Law and**
- **We think of God letting us off easy during this age of grace**

Let me give you a passage to make you rethink that a bit
Acts 17:30 KJV
And the times of this ignorance God winked at; but now commandeth all men every where to repent:

I do not want to make it sound like God is harsh and cruel today. But I do want to burst that false bubble that, since Jesus died on the cross, God is a teddy bear.

Remember Jesus said,
Matthew 10:34 KJV
Think not that I am come to send peace on earth: I came not to send peace, but a sword.

Remember also that,
The first time Jesus came as the Lamb of God
So peaceful was He that He would not even speak up to defend Himself.

The next time He comes it will be as the Lion of the Tribe of Judah.
The Bible says His vesture will be dipped in blood and a sharp sword goes out of His mouth.[75] This one-thousand-year kingdom of Jesus Christ that we often think of as Paradise on earth **will begin and end with a war**, and there is a terrible judgment[76] between them.

I will grant you that, by this time, those of us in this room who are saved, will be free from judgment. But it does serve to remind us that Christians today ARE called upon to
- **Be ready**
- **Walk worthy and**
- **Serve faithfully**

The Bible warns us that some people will go to heaven, saved yet so as by fire; saved but suffering loss.[77] But it also says that some will go to heaven with an abundant entrance.[78] So it does matter what sort of Christian life I live today. We don't all just go to heaven and find that the Lord has winked at all our sin. Even if we think we are getting away with it right now – we will then find out, too late to change it, that we were VERY wrong.

The thing is right now, I do have the opportunity to change all of that.
Ezekiel 18:21-22 KJV
But if the wicked will turn from all his sins that he hath committed, and keep all my statutes, and do that which is lawful and right, he shall surely live, he shall not die.

---

[75] Revelation 19:13-15
[76] The Valley of Jezreel
[77] 1 Corinthians 3:15 KJV
If any man's work shall be burned, he shall suffer loss: but he himself shall be saved; yet so as by fire.
[78] 2 Peter 1:11 KJV
For so an entrance shall be ministered unto you abundantly into the everlasting kingdom of our Lord and Saviour Jesus Christ.

All his transgressions that he hath committed, they shall not be mentioned unto him: in his righteousness that he hath done he shall live.

- **If we will hear the Word of God**
- **If we will turn away from the sin**
- **If we will give ourselves to following the way of God**

God promises that He won't remember those wicked things we have done.

During the one-thousand-year reign of the Lord
THE SAINTS WILL BE PERFECTED
Revelation 20:1-9 KJV

And I saw an angel come down from heaven, having the key of the bottomless pit and a great chain in his hand.

And he laid hold on the dragon, that old serpent, which is the Devil, and Satan, and bound him a thousand years,

And cast him into the bottomless pit, and shut him up, and set a seal upon him, that he should deceive the nations no more, till the thousand years should be fulfilled: and after that he must be loosed a little season.

And I saw thrones, and they sat upon them, and judgment was given unto them: and I saw the souls of them that were beheaded for the witness of Jesus, and for the word of God, and which had not worshipped the beast, neither his image, neither had received his mark upon their foreheads, or in their hands; and they lived and reigned with Christ a thousand years.

But the rest of the dead lived not again until the thousand years were finished. This is the first resurrection.

Blessed and holy is he that hath part in the first resurrection: on such the second death hath no power, but they shall be priests of God and of Christ, and shall reign with him a thousand years.

And when the thousand years are expired, Satan shall be loosed out of his prison,

And shall go out to deceive the nations which are in the four quarters of the earth, Gog and Magog, to gather them together to battle: the number of whom is as the sand of the sea.

And they went up on the breadth of the earth, and compassed the camp of the saints about, and the beloved city: and fire came down from God out of heaven, and devoured them.

A. The Thousand Year Reign of Christ is composed of three classes of people, with a fourth class coming along as the One Thousand Years goes on.

1. First, there are the New Testament saints like you and me.
The Bible says that we will rule and reign with Christ during this kingdom. We will have already been made perfect at the resurrection and rapture of those in Christ.[79]

2. Second there are those Old Testament and Tribulation Saints
They will also have already been made perfect through death and resurrection.[80]

---

[79] 1 Corinthians 15:50-54 KJV
Now this I say, brethren, that flesh and blood cannot inherit the kingdom of God; neither doth corruption inherit incorruption.
Behold, I shew you a mystery; We shall not all sleep, but we shall all be changed,
In a moment, in the twinkling of an eye, at the last trump: for the trumpet shall sound, and the dead shall be raised incorruptible, and we shall be changed.
For this corruptible must put on incorruption, and this mortal must put on immortality.
So when this corruptible shall have put on incorruption, and this mortal shall have put on immortality, then shall be brought to pass the saying that is written, Death is swallowed up in victory.
[80] Revelation 20:4-6 KJV
And I saw thrones, and they sat upon them, and judgment was given unto them: and I saw the souls of them that were beheaded for the witness of Jesus, and for the word of God, and which had not worshipped the beast, neither his image, neither had received his mark upon their foreheads, or in their hands; and they lived and reigned with Christ a thousand years.
But the rest of the dead lived not again until the thousand years were finished. This is the first resurrection.
Blessed and holy is he that hath part in the first resurrection: on such the second death hath no power, but they shall be priests of God and of Christ, and shall reign with him a thousand years.

3. Third, there are those Saints who got saved during and lived through the Tribulation.
These saints have not been perfected. Everyone who goes into the One Thousand Year Reign of Christ will be saved but they won't all be perfect.

- **That's why Christ rules with a rod of iron**
- **That's why we will rule and reign with Him**

We wouldn't have to have government and rules at all if no one had a sin nature. Government was not established by the Lord until after the Flood. Its only purpose is to manage the effects of the sin nature. Jesus will rule with a rod of iron and completely restrain the nature of sin for one thousand years.

The Bible also makes it clear that these same people will be having children.
- **We won't be having children**
- **Neither will the Old Testament saints**

But those who lived through the Tribulation will be able to have kids and will have them.

Now picture this:
- **Satan and his devils have been bound away**
- **The environment of the world is perfectly safe**
- **Government will be run by Jesus Christ Himself**
- **People will know exactly who God is and exactly what God wants**
- **Everyone to begin with will be saved**
- **No one will be allowed to sin**

but at the end of the one thousand years, Satan is loosed. And he is able to put together an army of people to fight against the Lord. It can't be any of those who lived through the Tribulation – they got saved way back then. It has to be their children.

And this answers all of the objections people have against faith today:

- **If I knew who God is I would follow Him**
- **If I saw Jesus personally I would believe in Him**
- **If I had not grown up in such a bad environment I would be a better person**
- **If my parents had raised me better I would not be in the trouble I am in**
- **If Satan had not tempted me, I would never have given in to sin**
- **If my government had taken better care of me I would have turned out better**

During the one thousand year reign of Christ the children born then will:
- **Have saved parents who are compelled to raise their kids right**
  - **No abuse**
  - **No neglect**
  - **No misplaced priorities**
- **Have the chance to see Jesus face to face**
- **Grow up not only worshipping God but worshipping God the right way**
- **None of them will have a bad experience**
  - **No friend will die in a tragic accident**
  - **Nobody will be crippled or maimed by some terrible event**
- **None of them will grow up in poverty and want**
- **Not one of them will ever be influenced by the devil to do the wrong thing**

And yet they are not automatically saved and inherently good. Those who follow the devil will be defeated. Everyone else will then be perfected. God's work of redemption will be completed.

The lesson I learn from the Millennial Kingdom is the necessity of personal salvation.

- **We don't need a better government**
- **We don't need to make parents raise their kids better**
- **We don't need to get our government to take better care of us**

What we need it to be saved; each and every one of us. Let's stop making excuses and let's get to the cross.

- **If you are not born again – today is the day to do so.**
- **If you are saved – stop making excuses for your sin and start walking with God**
- **If you have children – you can't make them be saved, but you can give them a shining example in your home, and you can pray for them.**

Chapter Twenty-Nine

THE COMING JUDGMENTS

Romans 14:7-12 KJV

For none of us liveth to himself, and no man dieth to himself.
For whether we live, we live unto the Lord; and whether we die, we die
unto the Lord: whether we live therefore, or die, we are the Lord's.
For to this end Christ both died, and rose, and revived, that he might be
Lord both of the dead and living.
But why dost thou judge thy brother? or why dost thou set at nought
thy brother? for we shall all stand before the judgment seat of Christ.
For it is written, As I live, saith the Lord, every knee shall bow to me,
and every tongue shall confess to God.
So then every one of us shall give account of himself to God.

A number of years ago a mother with several kids visited our services. Later that week she called me with a few questions about our church. It turned out that she lived about an hour and a half from here and because of a recent divorce from her husband, who was a deacon at the church she was coming from, was looking for another church to attend. She wanted it to be an independent Baptist Church and began to run through the usual questions I expect from someone interested in finding out more about our church.

But it turned out she had an agenda. She knew that one of our church doctrines would be what is often called "**Once Saved, Always Saved**". The doctrine teaches that a saved person can never, through sin or any circumstance, come to lose their salvation. And she came unglued when I affirmed my conviction of "once saved, always saved". Her husband had abused her, and she hated anyone and any church that believed he could still go to heaven after what he had done to her.

We Baptists have been accused of giving people a license to sin with that doctrine. To that accusation I give two defenses:
1. It isn't our doctrine, it is Bible teaching

- **Accuse the doctrine all you wish.**
- **Get angry at the messenger if you must**

but this doctrine is in the Bible and I have no right to preach anything other than what is in the Bible.

2. That isn't the whole story

There is, coming in the future of every man and woman, a judgment before God. As fierce as are the trials that people will face in the Tribulation:

- **Natural disasters**
- **Satanic persecution and**
- **The Battle of Armageddon**

in my mind none of these compare to that time when everyone of us shall give an account of himself to God.

- **The man who claims to be a Christian but has abused the grace of God and**
- **The man who has rejected Jesus Christ**

will each give an account of himself to God. A person might imagine that judgment to all happen at the same moment. But there are, in reality, three future judgments foretold in the Bible.

THE JUDGMENT SEAT OF CHRIST[81]

2 Corinthians 5:10-11 KJV

For we must all appear before the judgment seat of Christ; that every one may receive the things done in his body, according to that he hath done, whether it be good or bad.

---

[81] Romans 14:7-12 KJV

For none of us liveth to himself, and no man dieth to himself.
For whether we live, we live unto the Lord; and whether we die, we die unto the Lord: whether we live therefore, or die, we are the Lord's.
For to this end Christ both died, and rose, and revived, that he might be Lord both of the dead and living.
But why dost thou judge thy brother? or why dost thou set at nought thy brother? for we shall all stand before the judgment seat of Christ.
For it is written, As I live, saith the Lord, every knee shall bow to me, and every tongue shall confess to God.
So then every one of us shall give account of himself to God.

Knowing therefore the terror of the Lord, we persuade men; but we are made manifest unto God; and I trust also are made manifest in your consciences.

While the term is not found in the passage, I believe that 1 Corinthians 3:12-15 KJV describes that Judgment Seat of Christ,
Now if any man build upon this foundation gold, silver, precious stones, wood, hay, stubble;
Every man's work shall be made manifest: for the day shall declare it, because it shall be revealed by fire; and the fire shall try every man's work of what sort it is.
If any man's work abide which he hath built thereupon, he shall receive a reward.
If any man's work shall be burned, he shall suffer loss: but he himself shall be saved; yet so as by fire.

It appears to me that the Judgment Seat of Christ will take place immediately after the Rapture of all the Christians to heaven and the resurrection of those Christians who have died over the last two thousand years.

A couple of things to get drilled in our heads about this judgment:
A. It is a judgment of Christians
We sometimes forget (or choose to ignore) that there is such a thing as future judgment of Christians but I remind you that Peter said, 1 Peter 4:17 KJV
For the time is come that judgment must begin at the house of God: and if it first begin at us, what shall the end be of them that obey not the gospel of God?

So, there is a judgment of the Christians and it happens before any other judgment.

However,
B. It is not a judgment for sin
2 Corinthians 5:10 KJV

For we must all appear before the judgment seat of Christ; that every one may receive the things done in his body, according to that he hath done, whether it be good or bad.

Our sins have already been judged and forgiven because of the death of Jesus. Not that they are overlooked, but that they have been paid for. Jesus took our sins in His own body and suffered the judgment we should have for them. Our judgment is "according to that he hath done" in other words, our works as Christians.

Ephesians 2:10 KJV
For we are his workmanship, created in Christ Jesus unto good works, which God hath before ordained that we should walk in them.

God's will for the Christian is that we occupy ourselves with "good works." These are the things we will be judged over.

C. It is not a judgment for heaven or hell
The old picture of people standing at the pearly gates where Peter decides if we get to go into heaven or not is popular but not Bible.

The judgment seat of Christ happens in heaven, to Christians. Hell is already out of the question. However, it is still a judgment. Note the words:
- **Loss and**
- **Terror**

to them I will add another verse, 1 John 2:28 KJV
And now, little children, abide in him; that, when he shall appear, we may have confidence, and not be ashamed before him at his coming.

According to the Bible then, there will be people who go to heaven and, while thankfully saved, will experience **shame**.

I grew up rodeoing. My dad was a professional rodeo cowboy and we travelled a lot to the rodeos he was roping in.

But many weekends each year we were at amateur rodeos where I would race horses in timed events and ride bucking stock. I was pretty good on the horses and won lots of trophies and ribbons for those events. But I was never any good on the bucking events.

At a rodeo – professional or amateur, there is always an announcer's booth that sits up high above the area, keeping track of all that is going on. Inside the booth are several judges keeping track of times and scores. When the rodeo is over all of the cowboys would come onto the field where the announcers would announce to the crowd who the winners are.

I would usually get prizes for timed events, but only once or twice did I ever win anything in the bucking events.

Imagine they are announcing the winners of the bull riding.
- **Maybe a third-place ribbon went to Don Eckert**
- **Perhaps a second-place ribbon went to Nick Beeler**
- **Many times, the first place buckle went to Roho Raymand**

That would have been fine. But they never stopped there. They always announced the scores for everyone below them too. If I had gotten bucked off, I received no score so what the announcer would say to the crowd was "Let's give Marvin a round of applause. That's all he will get today."

I would rather have crawled in a hole than have them announce again that I got bucked off
- **I knew I got bucked off when I got bucked off**
- **All the other cowboys knew I got bucked off when I got bucked off**
- **Everyone in the bleachers saw me get bucked off when I got bucked off.**

Why do they have to bring it up again?

That's what the Judgment Seat of Christ will be like (only much more important).

THE VALLEY OF JEHOSHAPHAT
Joel 3:1-2 KJV

For, behold, in those days, and in that time, when I shall bring again the captivity of Judah and Jerusalem,
I will also gather all nations, and will bring them down into the valley of Jehoshaphat, and will plead with them there for my people and for my heritage Israel, whom they have scattered among the nations, and parted my land.

This is the least preached about and I think perhaps the most disturbing judgment to think upon. It happens after the Battle of Armageddon. Jesus returns to the earth with the armies of heaven in Revelation 19.

He fights the Battle of Armageddon with the beast and the false prophet.
- **The armies are destroyed**
- **The Beast and the False prophet are cast into the Lake of Fire and**
- **The dead are cast into hell**

According to the Bible Jesus' feet will touch down to earth on the Mount of Olives next to Jerusalem. He has come to set up His own kingdom. He will rule the earth for one thousand years with a rod of iron and He begins the work by gathering all nations to the Valley of Jehoshaphat, just southeast of Jerusalem.

I take it from other passages that the term nations here means everybody and not merely representatives from each nation. I understand it to mean that everyone who is alive at the end of the Tribulation Period
- **Those who are saved and escaped death at the hands of Antichrist and**
- **Those who are not saved and escaped death through natural disasters and the Battle of Armageddon**

Everyone alive on the earth at the end of the seven-year Tribulation will be summonsed to the Valley of Jehoshaphat just like Joseph and Mary were summonsed back to Bethlehem even though they lived in Nazareth and even though Mary was nine months pregnant. Everyone comes.

From here we can take up the description at the mouth of Jesus Christ:
Matthew 25:31-34 KJV
When the Son of man shall come in his glory, and all the holy angels with him, then shall he sit upon the throne of his glory:
And before him shall be gathered all nations: and he shall separate them one from another, as a shepherd divideth his sheep from the goats:
And he shall set the sheep on his right hand, but the goats on the left.
Then shall the King say unto them on his right hand, Come, ye blessed of my Father, inherit the kingdom prepared for you from the foundation of the world:

Matthew 25:41 KJV
Then shall he say also unto them on the left hand, Depart from me, ye cursed, into everlasting fire, prepared for the devil and his angels:

I understand this event to be at the Valley of Jehoshaphat. Everyone is lined up to be judged.
- **The saved as sheep are set on the right hand of Jesus to inherit the kingdom Jesus has come to establish.**
- **The lost as goats are place on his left hand to be cursed and cast into everlasting fire.**

How does it happen?
- **I think it is capital punishment.**
- **I think they are executed.**

- **When I man dies in combat that is one thing.**
- **But to be judged, found guilty and then executed – that is entirely different**

I am for capital punishment.
- **I believe it is necessary in a civilized world.**

- **I believe it is Biblically mandated**

But that doesn't mean I like capital punishment. I believe our nation ought to grieve every time it is necessary to put a person to death – no matter how terrible their crime.

Here is Jesus Christ –
- **The One who took upon Himself the sins of every one of these people lined up in the Valley**
- **The One who loves them so much that He died in their place**
- **The One whose blood is sufficient to have washed away every one of their sins**

And here He is called upon to order and enforce their executions.

When the Judgment at Jehoshaphat is finished, only those who are saved, "the sheep" remain to inherit the one-thousand-year reign of Jesus Christ.

THE GREAT WHITE THRONE JUDGMENT
Revelation 20:11-15 KJV

And I saw a great white throne, and him that sat on it, from whose face the earth and the heaven fled away; and there was found no place for them.

And I saw the dead, small and great, stand before God; and the books were opened: and another book was opened, which is the book of life: and the dead were judged out of those things which were written in the books, according to their works.

And the sea gave up the dead which were in it; and death and hell delivered up the dead which were in them: and they were judged every man according to their works.

And death and hell were cast into the lake of fire. This is the second death.

And whosoever was not found written in the book of life was cast into the lake of fire.

This Great White Throne Judgment is almost an exact opposite of the Judgment Seat of Christ.
- **Everyone there is unsaved**
- **Everyone there is judged for their sin**

- **Everyone there will go to hell and then the Lake of Faire and Brimstone**

Imagine for a moment the millions who now suffer the torments of hell.
- **Their minds are chafed**
- **Their tongues are parched**
- **Their bodies are twisted in agony**

Some of them have been in this misery for thousands of years with
- **No rest and**
- **No relief and**
- **No hope of respite**

In a moment, without warning – these souls who have rejected Jesus Christ as Saviour are reunited with their flesh and stand naked and exposed before God. There is no place for them to hide.

God the Bible says opens **The Book of Life**, also elsewhere called **The Lamb's Book of Life**.[82] It is the record of those who have received the gift of eternal life through Jesus Christ. But their names are not written there. I believe it is opened to demonstrate to them the justice of God's judgment upon them.

- **They could have received grace**
- **They could have been pardoned for the asking**

But they did not ask and now they will be judged out of the books. I believe those books are the books of the Bible, the Law.

Let me show you a couple of verses:
Galatians 3:12 KJV

---

[82] Revelation 21:27

And the law is not of faith: but, The man that doeth them shall live in them.

James 2:10 KJV
For whosoever shall keep the whole law, and yet offend in one point, he is guilty of all.

The Bible says that the man who chooses to practice the Law lives in the Law. Then it says that if you keep the whole Law very well, but break it in even one spot, you are judged as guilty of the whole thing. This Law doesn't have to be the Jewish Law, although it is the one referred to most of the time.

Romans 2:12-14 KJV
For as many as have sinned without law shall also perish without law: and as many as have sinned in the law shall be judged by the law;
(For not the hearers of the law are just before God, but the doers of the law shall be justified.
For when the Gentiles, which have not the law, do by nature the things contained in the law, these, having not the law, are a law unto themselves:

So, there is the Jewish Law, but there is also a natural law that every man knows instinctively – God put it in us. If we try to be good enough in our own power but fail even one time – even in the tiniest way. We become guilty of the who thing.

Those at the Great White Throne Judgment chose to try to live without Jesus Christ. They would forge their own way

- **They would practice religion or**
- **They would be good and moral or**
- **They would deny that there was such a judgment to come**

Their names were not written in The Book of Life, so they are judged instead to the fullest extent of the Law. They could have had mercy while in this life. But there will be no mercy at the **Great White Throne Judgment**.

Revelation 20:11 says there was found no place for them

- **There was found no place in the middle of the earth for them. It has been blasted out of existence**
- **There was found no place before God for them; they have rejected Christ as their Saviour**
- **There was found no place in heaven for them. Christ prepared a place for His own they are not His**

So, they are cast into the only place left; that place reserved for the devil and his angels. There they will suffer with him and without rest forever and forever and ever.

1 John 3:1-3 KJV
Behold, what manner of love the Father hath bestowed upon us, that we should be called the sons of God: therefore the world knoweth us not, because it knew him not.
Beloved, now are we the sons of God, and it doth not yet appear what we shall be: but we know that, when he shall appear, we shall be like him; for we shall see him as he is.
And every man that hath this hope in him purifieth himself, even as he is pure.

It is important that we hear messages like this because it is only through these types of messages that we are motivated to purify ourselves.

- **This isn't just religious talk**
- **This isn't a joke and**
- **This isn't so far away we don't have to worry about it right now**

This is serious business. Jesus is coming again. And when He comes – He will come with Judgment in His mind.

Chapter Thirty

ALL THINGS NEW

Revelation 21:1-5 KJV

And I saw a new heaven and a new earth: for the first heaven and the first earth were passed away; and there was no more sea.

And I John saw the holy city, new Jerusalem, coming down from God out of heaven, prepared as a bride adorned for her husband.

And I heard a great voice out of heaven saying, Behold, the tabernacle of God is with men, and he will dwell with them, and they shall be his people, and God himself shall be with them, and be their God.

And God shall wipe away all tears from their eyes; and there shall be no more death, neither sorrow, nor crying, neither shall there be any more pain: for the former things are passed away.

And he that sat upon the throne said, Behold, I make all things new. And he said unto me, Write: for these words are true and faithful.

When I began this segment having to do with last things that I gave what is the premise for calling prophetic messages fundamental or foundational to Christianity: "Our peace today rests on our faith in God's promises for the future."

Paul said,
Romans 8:18 KJV
For I reckon that the sufferings of this present time are not worthy to be compared with the glory which shall be revealed in us.

1 Corinthians 15:19 KJV
If in this life only we have hope in Christ, we are of all men most miserable.

Real Christianity is all about what awaits us in heaven. It's one of the great problems we have in modern Christianity – we have banked so heavily on happiness and blessings right here, right now, that we aren't willing to pay the price for treasures laid up in heaven instead of the earth. Here is the thing, our faith in God's promises are useless if we are only guessing what those promises are. That's why preaching and teaching about prophecy is fundamental doctrine.

- **It's more than pie in the sky in the sweet by and by**
- **It's bigger than some pleasant preaching to give us warm feelings**

It is the bedrock upon which a true Christian life is built. We have already looked at several of those promises:
- **The Rapture that rescues Christians from the Tribulation that will try the earth**
- **The Kingdom where we will rule as kings with Jesus Christ and**
- **The Judgment Seat of Christ where we will receive the treasures we have laid up in heaven**

We have all sorts of misguided and man-made ideas about what heaven will be like:
- **We become angels flying around with wings**
- **We only get our wings whenever a bell rings and**
- **Then we spend all of eternity playing our harp while sitting on a cloud**

That's not exactly the picture Revelation 21 paints for us.
THREE NEW THINGS
Revelation 21:1-2 KJV
And I saw a new heaven and a new earth: for the first heaven and the first earth were passed away; and there was no more sea.
And I John saw the holy city, new Jerusalem, coming down from God out of heaven, prepared as a bride adorned for her husband.

There are three new things mentioned in these two verses. They fit together to provide what will be eternity.

There is,
A. A New Heaven
A question comes to mind that goes something like this, "Why is a new heaven necessary?" and a couple of different answers have been postulated:
Some say this is speaking about outer space.

Remember how Paul wrote about the guy caught up to the third heaven?[83]

- **The first heaven is our atmosphere**
- **The second heaven is outer space**
- **The third heaven is where God's throne is**

These people say that man has polluted the second heaven with our space trash, and this is the heaven God will make new. I don't think that's it.[84] I think it is as simple as this – heaven, the place where God dwells, will be changed in the sense that **for the first since creation, man will be there and the devil will not**.

B. A New Earth

This one is blown into atoms just before the Great White Throne Judgment. Sinful man has done enough damage here.

- **We have just about exhausted the fresh water supplies**
- **We have just about exhausted the fresh air supplies**
- **We have just about used all of the oil supplies**
- **We have almost used up the forest supplies now**
- **We are covering the remaining free land with those ungodly looking wind mills**

But those are not, I think, what offends the Lord.

- **I think he put plenty of land on the earth for every human He planned to be here**
- **I am sure He made more than enough oil to fuel all the vehicles we will ever need**
- **There are enough trees, enough glaciers and enough systems in the air cycle to supply for all of mankind for all of man's time.**

---

[83] 2 Corinthians 12:2 KJV
I knew a man in Christ above fourteen years ago, (whether in the body, I cannot tell; or whether out of the body, I cannot tell: God knoweth;) such an one caught up to the third heaven.

[84] First, the passage doesn't specify the second heaven. The language and context imply God's heaven. Second the destruction of outer space is implied Revelation 20:11.

But there is one thing that can never be erased from this earth:

Genesis 4:10 KJV

And he said, What hast thou done? the voice of thy brother's blood crieth unto me from the ground.

The cry of Abel's blood, combined with that of a billion more:

- **Murdered by vile souls**
- **Brutalized over religious differences and**
- **Slaughtered in the battlefields of the world**

- **That, I believe, is the one thing that forever mars this land and**
- **That, I believe, is the one reason a new earth is necessary**

C. A New Jerusalem

What we usually think of as the Bible's description of heaven is really a description of the New Jerusalem:

- **The gates of pearl**
- **The walls of jasper**
- **The streets of gold**

All of that is in the New Jerusalem.

Revelation 21:10-19 KJV

And he carried me away in the spirit to a great and high mountain, and shewed me that great city, the holy Jerusalem, descending out of heaven from God,

Having the glory of God: and her light was like unto a stone most precious, even like a jasper stone, clear as crystal;

And had a wall great and high, and had twelve gates, and at the gates twelve angels, and names written thereon, which are the names of the twelve tribes of the children of Israel:

On the east three gates; on the north three gates; on the south three gates; and on the west three gates.

And the wall of the city had twelve foundations, and in them the names of the twelve apostles of the Lamb.

And he that talked with me had a golden reed to measure the city, and the gates thereof, and the wall thereof.

And the city lieth foursquare, and the length is as large as the breadth: and he measured the city with the reed, twelve thousand furlongs. The length and the breadth and the height of it are equal.
And he measured the wall thereof, an hundred and forty and four cubits, according to the measure of a man, that is, of the angel.
And the building of the wall of it was of jasper: and the city was pure gold, like unto clear glass.
And the foundations of the wall of the city were garnished with all manner of precious stones. ….

The old adage, "The devil is in the details" comes out to play again right here.

People argue about whether the city is the bride of Christ or the church is.
I think it is a foolish argument because neither is literally a bride but both are used figuratively as a bride.

People argue whether the city is cubed shape or pyramid shaped
The measurements given are true of either. I am not so worried about the shape as I am impressed about the size.

- **12,000 furlongs wide**
- **12,000 furlongs deeps and**
- **12,000 furlongs tall**

It is generally accepted that 12,000 furlongs would be about 1500 miles. That means that if you set this city on the West Coast of the United States it would stretch from:
- **San Diego, CA to Vancouver, BC (about 300 miles further into Canada)**
- **From San Francisco, Ca to Kansas City, MO**

I cannot tell you how the city is composed.
- **Is it more like a metropolis or a suburb?**
- **Does it have any countryside and open spaces?**
- **Is there something like Central Park in New York City?**
I do not know. I know it is ginormous.

Revelation 21 also lists what I am going to call,

NINE "NO" THINGS

Revelation 21:1-4 KJV

And I saw a new heaven and a new earth: for the first heaven and the first earth were passed away; and there was no more sea.

And I John saw the holy city, new Jerusalem, coming down from God out of heaven, prepared as a bride adorned for her husband.

And I heard a great voice out of heaven saying, Behold, the tabernacle of God is with men, and he will dwell with them, and they shall be his people, and God himself shall be with them, and be their God.

And God shall wipe away all tears from their eyes; and there shall be no more death, neither sorrow, nor crying, neither shall there be any more pain: for the former things are passed away.

Heaven can be defined as much for what is not there as for what is:

A. No Sea

Revelation 21:1 KJV

And I saw a new heaven and a new earth: for the first heaven and the first earth were passed away; and there was <u>no more sea</u>.

Remember that the oceans and the seas all came into being because of the Flood. To make a world without seas is to make a world that is paradise.

B. No death

Revelation 21:4 KJV

And God shall wipe away all tears from their eyes; and there shall be <u>no more death</u>, neither sorrow, nor crying, neither shall there be any more pain: for the former things are passed away.

My first thought is that this means no more fear

- **But it really means there is no more sin – the wages of sin is death.**
- **Sin, when it is finished bringeth forth death**

No death means there is no more consequence for sin – it is paid, and mortgage is burned.

C. No Sorrow
Revelation 21:4 KJV
And God shall wipe away all tears from their eyes; and there shall be no more death, <u>neither sorrow</u>, nor crying, neither shall there be any more pain: for the former things are passed away.

I love life. But I have reasons to sorrow:
- **The passing of my biological dad on Father's Day – he was not saved**
- **The failing health of my mom and stepdad I love very much**
- **The darkness of my sibling's lives without Christ**

Then there are the burdens I carry for people I pastor and others I consider brothers in the ministry.

I received a phone call from a pastor friend this week. He has been a pastor 45 years, I guess. But he has just been betrayed by an associate pastor who has been in his church 22 years. He has taken a sizable number from his church and started his own just down the road. He knew I would understand his pain and wanted to get some advice on how to deal with it.

D. No tears
Revelation 21:4 KJV
And <u>God shall wipe away all tears from their eyes</u>; and there shall be no more death, neither sorrow, <u>nor crying</u>, neither shall there be any more pain: for the former things are passed away.

There will be tears in heaven until after the Great White Throne:
- **Tears at the Judgment Seat when we suffer loss of rewards for our unfaithfulness to Christ**
- **Tears during the Tribulation as we witness souls suffering on this earth**
- **Tears at the end of the Thousand-year reign when Satan is loosed and puts together a final army against Christ and**
- **Tears at the Great White Throne when people we know, and love are judged and cast into the Lake of Fire and Brimstone**

But in eternity God does the miraculous. He wipes away those tears.

I do not know exactly what that means – I doubt that it means He will cause us to forget what happened in the past or what is happening in the Lake of Fire. In a way that is too high for us to imagine right now, God will wipe away the tears from our eyes.

E. No pain
Revelation 21:4 KJV
And God shall wipe away all tears from their eyes; and there shall be no more death, neither sorrow, nor crying, <u>neither shall there be any more pain</u>: for the former things are passed away.
- **Physical pain and**
- **Emotional pain**

is gone for good.

F. No temple
Revelation 21:22 KJV
And I saw no temple therein: for the Lord God Almighty and the Lamb are the temple of it.

This might seem like an unusual feature but remember what the temple represented: it was a bridge so that sinful man had a way to reach out to God. There will be no need for that bridge in eternity. We will have free access to God and the Jesus.

G. No sun
Revelation 21:23 KJV
And the city <u>had no need of the sun</u>, neither of the moon, to shine in it: for the glory of God did lighten it, and the Lamb is the light thereof.

We can't live without the sun, but we also have to be protected from the sun. In eternity we have Jesus Christ who is our life – and nothing negative at all.

H. No night
Revelation 21:25 KJV

And the gates of it shall not be shut at all by day: for <u>there shall be no night there.</u>

The passage makes its own interpretation. Absolute safety in heaven.

All of this, I think is summed up in on final "no" thing

I. No curse

Revelation 22:3 KJV

And there shall be no more curse: but the throne of God and of the Lamb shall be in it; and his servants shall serve him:

The curse of sin is what make all of the above bad.

- **No sin**
- **No curse**
- **No death, crying, pain or sorrows**

I almost feel like I should apologize for what I am about to say.

ONE WARNING

Revelation 21:27 KJV

And there shall <u>in no wise enter</u> into it any thing that defileth, neither whatsoever worketh abomination, or maketh a lie: but they which are written in the Lamb's book of life.

Don't we love to preach everyone into heaven? Wouldn't it be great if,

- **Every person we have ever loved**
- **Every member of our family**
- **Every friend**
- **Every colleague**

Went to heaven no matter what the believed?

A few years ago, I was approached by a man who had graduated from Pacific Coast Baptist Bible College. Although he had never been a pastor, his family asked if he would officiate his grandmother's funeral. He came to me with two questions

- **First, he needed help organizing the funeral service – the technical stuff**
- **Second, he needed help reconciling his love for his grandmother with the Bible fact that she, as an unbeliever, did not go to heaven**

He did the service as his family requested, but then quit church. When I visited with him his answer was bluntly that he didn't want to worship a God who would not let his grandmother into heaven just because she didn't ask Jesus to save her.

I am afraid I have to tell you that I do not have the authority to whitewash or explain this verse away; no real preacher does. Here is the plain truth of the Bible; no one enters into heaven unless their name is in the Lamb's Book of Life.

No one goes to heaven unless there was a time when

- **They became convicted of their sin**
- **They realized their sin would condemn them to eternal hell**
- **They sensed the call of God to trust Jesus Christ and**
- **They responded to that call by repenting of their sins and turning to the Lord Jesus Christ**

No one goes to heaven unless they have obeyed the gospel and gotten saved.

Chapter Thirty-One

WHEN IT'S ALL SAID AND DONE
Revelation 22:6-21 KJV

And he said unto me, These sayings are faithful and true: and the Lord God of the holy prophets sent his angel to shew unto his servants the things which must shortly be done.

<u>Behold, I come quickly</u>: blessed is he that keepeth the sayings of the prophecy of this book.

And I John saw these things, and heard them. And when I had heard and seen, I fell down to worship before the feet of the angel which shewed me these things.

Then saith he unto me, See thou do it not: for I am thy fellowservant, and of thy brethren the prophets, and of them which keep the sayings of this book: worship God.

And he saith unto me, Seal not the sayings of the prophecy of this book: for the time is at hand.

He that is unjust, let him be unjust still: and he which is filthy, let him be filthy still: and he that is righteous, let him be righteous still: and he that is holy, let him be holy still.

And<u>, behold, I come quickly;</u> and my reward is with me, to give every man according as his work shall be.

I am Alpha and Omega, the beginning and the end, the first and the last.

Blessed are they that do his commandments, that they may have right to the tree of life, and may enter in through the gates into the city.

For without are dogs, and sorcerers, and whoremongers, and murderers, and idolaters, and whosoever loveth and maketh a lie.

I Jesus have sent mine angel to testify unto you these things in the churches. I am the root and the offspring of David, and the bright and morning star.

And the Spirit and the bride say, Come. And let him that heareth say, Come. And let him that is athirst come. And whosoever will, let him take the water of life freely.

For I testify unto every man that heareth the words of the prophecy of this book, If any man shall add unto these things, God shall add unto him the plagues that are written in this book:

And if any man shall take away from the words of the book of this prophecy, God shall take away his part out of the book of life, and out of the holy city, and from the things which are written in this book.

He which testifieth these things saith, <u>Surely I come quickly</u>. Amen. Even so, come, Lord Jesus.

The grace of our Lord Jesus Christ be with you all. Amen.

When we think of the book of the Revelation of Jesus Christ, we generally think about Apostle John being taken in the Spirit into heaven to see things that will happen in the future. But the book neither begins nor ends in heaven.

The first three chapters find John exiled – suffering persecution for his faith. In chapter four he is carried away in the Spirit to heaven and to future things but with Revelation chapter 22, we find the Apostle John coming:
- **Back into the present**
- **Back to earth and**
- **Back to the isle of Patmos, where he was exiled**

He has seen some terrible things in the future:
- **The supernatural disasters of the Tribulation**
- **The unbridled persecution of the Antichrist and**
- **The Great White Throne Judgment**

But He has also seen some wonderful things:
- **God's throne in heaven**
- **The millennial kingdom of Christ and**
- **Eternal happiness**

He must have felt something like we do when we come home from a vacation:
- **We were in a wonderful place**
- **We had no real cares or worries**
- **We got to forget real life**

But when we get home – everything is just like it was when we left.

John had the blessing of seeing the future but when he came back down to earth – everything was just like it was before he saw his vision. But I am glad that the Lord didn't drop him off too suddenly. As John moved from his heavenly vision back into the world of now, Jesus Christ gave a promise and repeated it three times.

That promise is the final fundamental doctrine. Three times Jesus promised, "*I come quickly.*"

- **Vs 7**
- **Vs 12**
- **Vs 20**

The most basic, the most fundamental doctrine of prophecy is this promise of Jesus:
Behold, I come quickly.

Not just that He will come as He promised in,
John 14:3 KJV
And if I go and prepare a place for you, I will come again, and receive you unto myself; that where I am, there ye may be also.

Not just that He will come the same way He left as we are told in,
Acts 1:11 KJV
… this same Jesus, which is taken up from you into heaven, shall so come in like manner as ye have seen him go into heaven.

The promise is
- **That He will come quickly**
- **That it won't be very long from now**
- **That it will happen sooner than any of us think**

There is first,
AN INVITATION
Vs 12-17

When a person really begins to analyze the Bible as a whole I think we could say that its whole purpose is to give an invitation. God's message from Genesis chapter one to Revelation chapter twenty-two is the same: "**Come**"
- **Come if you are thirsty**
- **Come if you are needy**
- **Come if you hear Him calling**

Come!

There is no cost to come to Christ – you may freely take what He offers. There are no conditions to come to Christ – whosoever will may come. God has been drawing men out of this world and to Himself since there were men cursed with the disease of sin:

- **He called Abraham out of the Ur of Chaldees to a place God shewed Him**
- **He called Moses out of the desert to lead Israel out of slavery**
- **He called David out of the fields of a shepherd to be the king of his people**
- **He called Daniel to be a light in the darkness of Babylon**
- **He called Peter and James and John and the other Apostles to be the foundation for His church**

- **He called Saul of Tarsus from his religious frustration to be a witness to the Gentile nations**

And still He is calling men and women to come to Him.

- **He called my wife at a teen youth rally**
- **He called me through a TV preacher**

- **He called some of you while you were just children**
- **He called others of you as full adults**

And if you are not saved today

- **He is calling you to come to Him.**

Our world has confused the whole doctrine of salvation so that some people haven't gotten saved because they think they could not measure up.

The fact is that getting saved is a wonderfully easy thing to do. Someone has observed that it is
As easy as drinking a sip of water
Revelation 22:17 KJV
… And let him that is athirst come. And whosoever will, let him take the water of life freely.

As easy as answering the door
Revelation 3:20 KJV
Behold, I stand at the door, and knock: if any man hear my voice, and open the door, I will come in to him, and will sup with him, and he with me.

As easy as asking a simple question
Romans 10:13 KJV
"Whosoever shall call upon the name of the Lord shall be saved."

There is nothing preventing any person from being saved by the grace of God except their own lack of willingness.
Revelation 22:17 says,
Whosoever will, let him take….

Jesus promises He is coming quickly and invites us to be saved.

A WARNING
Vs 7-11, 18

As it is found in this chapter, that warning takes on two parts:
A. You must come to the Lord the Bible way
Revelation 22:18-19 KJV
For I testify unto every man that heareth the words of the prophecy of this book, If any man shall add unto these things, God shall add unto him the plagues that are written in this book:
And if any man shall take away from the words of the book of this prophecy, God shall take away his part out of the book of life, and out of the holy city, and from the things which are written in this book.[85]

---

[85] The most common way to interpret this passage is to speak of those who change the Bible through corrupt translations. While this is a completely acceptable interpretation, I offer a secondary one in this message.

When it comes to faith, one of the biggest mistakes people make is to assume they can come any way they please, so long as they come.

A read a quote last week from a famous Protestant preacher Martin Lloyd-Jones. It read, **"We must remember that equally honest men may differ."** I responded by saying, **"The test God places before us is truth, not honesty."**

The Bible says in,
John 4:24 KJV
God is a Spirit: and they that worship him must worship him in spirit and in truth.

It does not say, "…in spirit and in honesty." A person can be completely honest and not know the truth. That's the problem with religion. It attempts to come to God some way other than by the truth of God's Word. Like the Muslims who see Jesus as one of the prophets but not *the* Saviour, religion sees the Bible as one way to know the truth but not *the* way to know the truth. Because they won't take the Bible at face value, they miss salvation altogether.

B. You must come to Jesus before Jesus comes for you
Revelation 22:11 KJV
He that is unjust, let him be unjust still: and he which is filthy, let him be filthy still: and he that is righteous, let him be righteous still: and he that is holy, let him be holy still.

I am reminded of,
Luke 12:16-21 KJV
And he spake a parable unto them, saying, The ground of a certain rich man brought forth plentifully:
And he thought within himself, saying, What shall I do, because I have no room where to bestow my fruits?
And he said, This will I do: I will pull down my barns, and build greater; and there will I bestow all my fruits and my goods.
And I will say to my soul, Soul, thou hast much goods laid up for many years; take thine ease, eat, drink, and be merry.

But God said unto him, Thou fool, this night thy soul shall be required of thee: then whose shall those things be, which thou hast provided?
So is he that layeth up treasure for himself, and is not rich toward God.

None of us knows when our soul will be required of us. That is why making things right with God ought to begin right now. Jesus promised, *"Behold, I come quickly."* So "**quickly**" is the way to get right with the Lord.

Hebrews 3:7-8 KJV
Wherefore (as the Holy Ghost saith, To day if ye will hear his voice,
Harden not your hearts, as in the provocation, in the day of temptation in the wilderness:
- **Not tomorrow, giving the devil the chance to rob you of the conviction God is building in your soul right now**
- **Not later, when you think it will be more convenient**

The Bible says "Today"
- **Hear His voice "today"**
- **Come to Him "today"**
- **Turn from your sin "today"**

If you have not trusted Christ as Saviour, then do so, "today."

So, we see first of all in the promise that Jesus is coming quickly
- **An invitation – come to Him second**
- **A warning – come the Bible way and come today**

A LONGING
Vs 20

Remember the situation right here. John is coming:
- **Back into real time**
- **Back down to the Island of Patmos**
- **Back to the pressures of exile and persecution**

He had gotten a taste of heaven, but he didn't get to stay there.

- **He had seen the streets of gold**
- **He had witnessed of world of no sickness death or pain**
- **He had bathed in the light of Jesus Christ**

But it wasn't his reality – yet.

- **Reality was where every one of his fellow Apostles was executed**
- **Reality was where sickness, suffering, pain and death was a daily event**

In heaven the tree of life "*...bare twelve manner of fruits and yielded her fruit every month.*"[86]

Reality was that men were still earning their bread by the sweat of their face.
- **In heaven there is rest**
- **In reality there was still hard work**

I realize my illustration is trivial when compared to what Apostle John must have experienced but it reminds me of coming home from a fantastic vacation.
- **Somewhere warm**
- **Somewhere that everyone around us was there to help us**
- **Somewhere that every meal is fixed by someone else**

But then the car pulls into the driveway
- **The bills have been piling up, waiting for you to come home**
- **The lawn has been growing and now its going to be a pain to mow**
- **There is a message from work and you'll have a problem to fix when you get back on Monday**

And before you lay your head down on your pillow that first night home from vacation you think, "I can't wait to go on vacation again." I do not mean to make light of the situation

---

[86] Revelation 22:2

in Revelation but just to give you a bit of the sense that John must have been feeling after his vision of the future.

The vision is over but, in those words, *"Behold, I come quickly,"* Jesus promises Him it will all happen soon.
- **He hears Jesus in verse 7, *"Behold, I come quickly."***
- **He hears him again in verse 12, *"Behold, I come quickly."***
- **He hears him the third time in verse 20, *"Surely I come quickly."***

And this time he breaths out His heart's longing, *"Even so, come, Lord Jesus."*

May I say that every Christian has the right to breath that very same prayer.

Even so – as you have promised
Even so- as a thief in the night
Even so- to call your children to heaven

Come–to this earth
Come - for your believers
Come-to rescue us from these trials

Lord Jesus – not an apostle or a representative from the dead
Lord Jesus- not an angel, even if it is Gabriel
Lord Jesus – Yourself, personally

- **Come in your glorified body**
- **Come as the Lion of the Tribe of Judah**
- **Come to be King of kings and Lord of lords**

And Bible says, Titus 2:13 KJV says
Looking for that blessed hope, and the glorious appearing of the great God and our Saviour Jesus Christ;

Jesus is coming – quickly.
1 John 3:1-3 KJV

Behold, what manner of love the Father hath bestowed upon us, that we should be called the sons of God: therefore the world knoweth us not, because it knew him not.

Beloved, now are we the sons of God, and it doth not yet appear what we shall be: but we know that, when he shall appear, we shall be like him; for we shall see him as he is.

And every man that hath this hope in him purifieth himself, even as he is pure.

A plea for mercy

I beseech thee, dear reader, for mercy. I am aware of my deficiencies in grammar, punctuation and typing. I humbly confess I know not the depth of my weakness in these areas. Being but a simple preacher with a love for writing, I do not possess the resources for adequate proofreading and editing. Please forgive the egregious blunders.

If there has been some small part of this book that has helped you, I count that a great blessing from our Lord.

Should you find the book is helpful to you, or if you have questions you would like to ask me, feel free to contact me. My e-mail address is pastormck@bbcpuyallup.org.

Made in the USA
Monee, IL
10 January 2024

51514272R10166